"It's like having a great conversation with someone who you love. It's so unassuming. It lets you know that even if you're trying a little bit, you're doing wonderfully well. It absolves you of the need to show off. That brings that wonderful attitude of like, 'Why shouldn't you try making jam? Make jam! If it doesn't work, who cares?' It's not like your life revolves around success or failure with making jams. Just try it—you don't ever have to do it again. I find it very relaxing." —Samantha Bee

"When I think of good writing about food I always think first of the immortal Laurie Colwin. . . . Colwin's unpretentious essays about whipping up the likes of buttered noodles and savory beef stew are collected in two books: *Home Cooking* and *More Home Cooking*." —Maureen Corrigan, NPR's *Fresh Air*

"A treatise on the importance of the family dinner—no matter who you consider to be family."

—*The Guardian*, "Top 10 Culinary Memoirs"

"Every winter, after the frenzy of the holidays has died down, I reread the late Laurie Colwin's *Home Cooking* and *More Home Cooking*. They're two of the friendliest, chattiest, most approachable books I've ever read, and among the top tier of works that informed my own sensibility as a cook. . . . Her self-deprecating accounts of meals cobbled together in a shoebox-size Manhattan apartment and her full-throated approach to feeding her family never fail to inspire me when I'm all cooked out. This year, I felt like I'd just put down my well-worn copies when I picked them right up again, craving nothing but the reassuring voice of an old friend—a cake baker, a bread maker, a fan of simple fare and the tried and true." —*Salon*

"When you read an author who writes like someone's in the room talking to you, you can't help but fall in love, which is what a huge audience did in the 1970s when Laurie Colwin appeared in *The New Yorker*, *Gourmet* magazine, and *Mademoiselle*. . . . She is witty and frank and fun."　　　　　*—Boston Globe*

"When the impeccable novelist-of-manners Laurie Colwin died unexpectedly in 1992 at the age of forty-eight, her readers felt they had lost their best friend. As a writer, she was even better than a best friend, amusing and affirming, not the kind who secretly competed with you or called only when she wanted something. . . . What I recommend most highly is her classic book of essays and recipes, *More Home Cooking*. *Home Cooking* is tasty, but in this second volume, she goes even deeper, generously serving up her last words."　　*—Sarasota Herald-Tribune*

"A novelist with a love for food, Colwin writes with a cozy style that invites you in, sits you down, and serves you tea. The author's recipes come from her own experiences, some from hard-won battles in the kitchen. Unpretentious and enthusiastic, with a love of comfort, Colwin coaxes you to attempt a new recipe, even if it's intimidating and even if you fail."

—Los Angeles Magazine

"The first time I read Laurie Colwin, I knew I'd found the friend I'd always wanted to join me in the kitchen. Warm, funny, and unpretentious, she made me laugh and made me want to cook. Her recipes were easy and delicious. All these years later, when I'm feeling sad, or wondering what to cook, I turn to Laurie Colwin. And she never lets me down."

—Ruth Reichl, author of Save Me the Plums

"Filled with essays about food, family, and life. . . . Her writing is a treat. . . . It's a joy to read—the kind of work that makes you want to get cooking yourself." —*Boston Phoenix*

"We all need a best friend when we are at home cooking; this is the next best thing." —*Seattle Weekly*

"Colwin's writing is down-to-earth and friendly, as though she is presenting little morsels she has prepared just for you. There are no frills or tricks. Like a classic dish, her writing's magic in its simplicity." —*Charlotte Observer*

"To her devoted readers—and there are many—writer Laurie Colwin's tastes and habits are nearly as familiar as their own. . . . Colwin's voice is warm and bossy and prescriptive in the most comforting way possible. . . . She will assure you that everything will turn out fine, even if dinner itself turns out to be a disaster. She knows, because she has had spectacular failures in the kitchen and has survived to share them." —*Chicago Reader*

"Foodies and readers: you must know Laurie Colwin . . . the best writer you've never heard of, let alone read. . . . All of Colwin's writing has that timeless quality I associate with great literature, particularly when she's musing about food. . . . Superb, insightful writing." —*The Tyee* (British Columbia)

"Laurie Colwin teaches us how to cook, eat, deal with disasters, write, and live. We turn to her books for a kind of comfort and sustenance that only she can provide."
—Emily Gould, author of *Friendship* and *Perfect Tunes*

MORE HOME COOKING

ALSO BY LAURIE COLWIN

Novels

Shine On, Bright and Dangerous Object
Happy All the Time
Family Happiness
Goodbye Without Leaving
A Big Storm Knocked It Over

Stories

Passion and Affect
The Lone Pilgrim
Another Marvelous Thing

Essays

Home Cooking

MORE HOME COOKING

A Writer Returns to the Kitchen

LAURIE COLWIN

Foreword by Deb Perelman

HARPER ● PERENNIAL

NEW YORK ● LONDON ● TORONTO ● SYDNEY ● NEW DELHI ● AUCKLAND

HARPER ● PERENNIAL

Portions of this text were originally published in *Gourmet* magazine.

A HARDCOVER EDITION OF THIS BOOK WAS PUBLISHED IN 1993 BY HARPER-COLLINS PUBLISHERS.

FIRST HARPER PERENNIAL EDITION PUBLISHED IN 1995.
REVISED EDITION PUBLISHED IN 2000.
REISSUED IN HARPER PERENNIAL IN 2014, 2021.

Based on a design by Virginia Tan

The Library of Congress has catalogued the hardcover edition as follows:
    Colwin, Laurie.
    More home cooking: a writer returns to the kitchen / Laurie Colwin.
    p. cm.
    ISBN 0-06-016849-8
    1. Entertaining. 2. Cookery. I. Title.
    TX652.C7143   1993
642'.4—dc20   93-29184

ISBN 978-0-06-304642-9 (pbk.)

HB 06.07.2024

For Jeanne Heifetz and Rick Kot

ACKNOWLEDGMENTS

I would like to thank some pals with whom I have broken bread and talked about life and what sustains it.

At *Gourmet*: Lorraine Alexander, Jan Daniels, Kathleen Duffy Freund, Kalli Ide, Hobby McKenney, Alexis Touchet, Gail Zeigenthal, and Alice Gochman.

In New York City: Linda Faulhaber, Stewart Fishman, Karen Edwards and Michael Ellis, Alice Quinn, Cynthia B. Elitzer, Janet Checkman, Franny Taliaferro, Rob Wynne and Charles Ruas, Carol Shookoff, Aimee Garn, the brothers Thanhauser, Candida Donadio and Eric Ashworth, Arthur Randall, Jeannette Kossuth, Anna Shapiro, Nancy Crampton, Seymour Britchky, Vicky Wilson, Pat Strachan ("aka Pat S., not her real name"), Peggy Resnick, Inez Fontenez, Anna Forrester, Carol Santangelo and David "Howling Wolf" Hunt, Sheila Gillooly, Bapsi Sidhwa, Christine Pittel, Blair Brown, Margaret Diehl, Dee Eisenberg and Wally Shawn, Audra Herman, Rivilyn Zweig, Jenny Feder and Jill Dunbar, John Westermann, Peter Derrick and Jan Molnar, Eleanor Larrabee, Ray Pierce, Charles Rohrs, Carol and Peter Howell, Gus Mortada and Jose Bruno, Frank and Mommy, Yehuda Nir and Bonnie Maslin, Scott Spencer, Alan and Laura Hruska, Roger Friedman, Miki Allen, Susan Bergholz and Burt Snyder, Eddie Torres, Danny Zitin, Bob Hayes, Jerry Corsini, Mindy Pennybacker, and the world's best upstairs neighbors, Susan and Rodney Gabel.

In West Cornwall: Janice and Don Bracken, Julie Devlin, Earl Brecker, Ann and Ralph Gold, David and Alice Cadwell, Katherine Perry and Sean White, Betsy Osha, Lee Taliaferro, Evelyn and Jessie Gelerter, Jill Cutler and Jeremy Brecker, Mary O'Brien, Gordon Ridgeway, Mary Lee, Barbara Farnsworth, Sue Kochman and Paul Wiske.

In Philadelphia: Jane Bibberman, Leslie and Jerry Rivkin.

In Baltimore: Jonathan Yardley.

In Iowa: Jim Harris.

In California: Gene and Sylvia Thompson, Connie Casey, Sparky Schulz, Don and Marilyn Sipes, Ronnie Roose, Nicky Meyer, Jeff and Judy Barber, Debbie Rheinish, and Esther Mitgang.

In Texas: Willard Spiegelman and the Flying Orlovskys.

In Bogotá: Dr. Carlos Hecht.

In Beijing: Joan Pinkham.

In London: Juliet Annan, Sylvie Herold and Ib Bellew, Margaret Welles, the Armstrongs, Sue Fletcher, Hugh Fleetwood, and Richard Davies.

And with me everywhere and always: Rosa.

CONTENTS

FOREWORD

Nobody makes you feel more at home in the kitchen than Laurie Colwin. Her unfussy writing is a balm for kitchen skeptics, and a welcome mat laid out for people who spend a lot of time, borderline-too-much time (if you ask their friends and family) thinking about food and cooking. Her utter lack of pretension, of self-puffery, is enviable and particularly stands out today, when cooks are also supposed to be public figures with social media strategies and good lighting. Her charm and empathy resonate through every reminder of "I assure you that if you keep it simple, everything will turn out just fine."

I suspect Colwin is not for everyone. Not everyone starts thinking about what to make for dinner the minute they finish breakfast. Not everyone plans their weekend around a cooking whim they got from a novel they read. Not everyone keeps cookbooks on their bedside table. Not everyone is delighted by an essay about how great lemons are or the perfect meal to serve a jetlagged friend, or is charmed by the idea of eating nursery food as an adult. But for those of us who do, Colwin normalizes all the ways we once thought we were odd.

"What is more interesting than how people live?" she asks in one of my favorite essays in this book, "Why I Love Cookbooks." "Maybe war, or death or something, but not to me. I like to know how they serve food, what they do with it, how it looks."

Colwin knows that food people aren't obsessed with sustenance per se, they just see it as the prism through which everything else makes sense. She knows that talking about food is the safest way one can be nosy without being rude, because what we're really asking when we ask what a friend ate for dinner is: Who came over, what was their favorite thing you made, did they help with the dishes, are they invited back, did you get any good gossip, wait, what do you mean they don't like soup, who doesn't like soup?

This is how it was for me when I first read *Home Cooking* and *More Home Cooking*, a year or so after starting a food blog with the hope of finding my people, the kind who wouldn't mind that I'd go on for twenty minutes when I was asked the difference between summer and winter squash, expounding on why I totally understand why a lot of people find them bland but it's just that they need to make them in one of my four favorite ways, described in detail with a sidebar about the zucchini butter spaghetti I hadn't gotten right yet, but promised to soon. In Colwin's writing, I found the friendlier, approachable voice I wished more food writing channeled. Wasn't cooking winter squash for the first time scary enough? Why lecture when you can gently guide?

I knew she'd passed away far too young, nearly fifteen years before I discovered her work, but I didn't expect everything she'd written to be so relatable that it would feel like it could have been written fifteen minutes ago. So many of her ideas about food are still so current, including her advocacy for buying locally and eating seasonally. She wants our dinner tables to be less old-fashioned and more inclusive of the way real families look: divorced, remarried, from mixed backgrounds, and more, a message as welcome in 1993 and it is in 2021. She understands frugality on a visceral level, discouraging the use of brisket for her boiled beef recipe because there are better ways to cook a child's college fund.

Despite her love for food and cooking, these aren't just frivolous meanderings. There's something very no-nonsense about her writing, whether she deadpans in the introduction that "Most people who intend to have a family meal are too busy to think about the cultural relevance of this fact," and that's just page one. Is she wryly looking inward? Is this the perfect jab at us with the privilege to not just consume food, but to analyze it? Is she telling us she's in on the joke, too? It catches me off guard every time I read it, but it also ushers me into a collection that feels as relevant to the way we cook, and live, now as it did decades ago.

She wants us to worry less, enjoy things more, in the kitchen. Colwin is passionate about dinner party menus that are easy but that you can be proud of, the kind she outlines in "After the Holidays." If you're feeling overwhelmed, she wants you to know that she suspects that the adults in the perfect-looking family in Norman Rockwell's Thanksgiving painting probably had a few bitter words in the kitchen about in-laws, or that she resents doing all of the clean-up. She calls black beans "a frazzled person's friend," in a recipe for a black bean soup that several *Smitten Kitchen* readers have told me is a forever favorite, because black bean soup never goes out of style.

Colwin is keenly interested in helping you make the kinds of decisions inside the kitchen that will give you a good life outside of it, from astonishingly good bread that doesn't lock your day to a strict schedule of kneading, rising, and deflation, to the black bean soup that simmers for five hours, allowing you time to yak on the phone to a friend, play with a child, or go shopping for yourself. She always offers a suggestion for how she'd expand on a dish to include friends coming by at the last minute, the kind of impulsivity that sounds positively decadent after a year of social distancing.

But mostly, she wants you to know that cooking is for everyone. You don't need to be a chef genius or come from a long culinary tradition to prepare food, she tells us in "Plain Food." You just need to eat something, decide you like it, ask the person who made it how they did it, and take this information back to your own kitchen. She's anti-soufflé and pro–simple cake; anti-trussing and pro–trusting your gut, and I bet she'd be absolutely thrilled we are still here, delighting in her timeless encouragement.

—*Deb Perelman*
June 2021

MORE HOME COOKING

Introduction

The Family Dinner in Real Life

Let us sit down and talk straight about the family dinner, that supposed artifact of years gone by. It is said that these days (in contrast to those days, when families gathered together for at least their evening meal), the family meal has vanished, and what we now are left with is The Snack. No one sits down with anyone anymore. We are a nation, we are told, of people who eat pizza or yogurt on the run, and standing up.

Most people who intend to have a family meal are too busy to think about the cultural relevance of this act. The fact is that modern life has deprived us of life's one great luxury: time. In the old days things *were* different. Mom was home, Dad at work, the kids in school. When the old Dodge pulled into the driveway (or as the old Dodge pulled away from the railroad station with Dad inside and Mom driving and the kids in the back) dinner was ready, and then, it is imagined, a cheerful meal was had by all.

Now, of course, everyone works. The morning does not feature a communal breakfast with bacon and eggs and oatmeal (no one eats bacon and eggs anymore, in any case) and the morning is a scramble to get Mom and Dad into their work clothes, children into their snowsuits, lunch boxes packed, and the house pulled together. It is no wonder we look back nostalgically on those supposed heavenly days of yore.

It is my opinion that Norman Rockwell and his ilk have done more to make already anxious people feel guilty than anyone else. I myself am reduced to worm size when contemplating his famous illustration of the farm family Thanksgiving table, with the beaming grandparents and the children with their hair combed. How happy they all look! And how politely and still the children sit! Why can't I get my child to sit like that? And when her cousins come to a family dinner, why do they all *wander* so much? And when I gaze at Norman Rockwell's enchanting Thanksgiving picture, why do I suspect that the grandfather drinks more than he should, that the mother and father have had a few bitter words in the kitchen about the in-laws, or the mom has told the dad how much she resents doing all the cooking when all he has done is watch the football game and never so much as poke his head into the kitchen to ask if she needed help, and that the aunt is taking either antidepressants or mood elevators?

The fact is, family is variable, but our stereotypical image of it is not. And so as we sit to our family tables, with our children wandering and our table full of family we are on dicey terms with, we are still hag-ridden by the image of the happy, harmonious, white, two-parent family. We would all be a lot happier if we could relax a little and have some fun. We must sweep away these old, ingrained images and lighten up: The world is full of possibilities.

Let us imagine a family table. Some of the people sitting at it are blood relatives and some are family by choice. After all, what do we mean by family? We mean people who are deeply and lovingly connected to one another (for better and worse), people we can count on. In a pinch I can call my sister. I can also call on one of my close old pals who is related to me by bonds, and bonds can be every bit as strong as blood, just as blood can be much less consequential than a bond.

Here at the table is a single mother with an adopted child from El Salvador. Also her beau, the divorced father of two. Also their mutual friends, a female couple who have successfully raised together the son of one of the women. (These families are hell on grammar.) The single mother, who was raised an Orthodox Jew, has a bunch of nieces and nephews who are the products of a Jewish mother and a Moslem father from Pakistan, and the children grew up in Mexico and naturally speak Spanish as well as Urdu.

Then mix in some family by choice: the oldest friend, her husband and daughter, a friend of the oldest friend (and godmother to the oldest friend's daughter), and the oldest friend's friend's beau, who is from Shanghai, plus a stray English visitor who spent five minutes viewing this mob in a kind of dazed state and then put her feet up with everyone else.

This is the description of a festive meal: Thanksgiving, or Passover, or Christmas. But everyday life is something else again— our nuclear families flying off in different directions, faced with daily challenges of all sorts and not a moment to rest, re-create, and dine.

These are hard times for people who like to eat, who like to cook, and who hate to do both but need to. Our present economic system leaves us pressed, drained, exhausted, and yet . . . and yet we still need sustenance, and contact. We need time to defuse, to contemplate. Just as in sleep our brains relax and give us dreams, so at some time in the day we need to disconnect, reconnect, and look around us.

Life these days does not leave much room for this sort of thing. Some people have never been taught to cook, or taught to eat. When I was a little girl, children sat at the table with their parents when they were old enough to take part in what you might call "table life." You had to be able to manage your knife and fork. You needed to practice your table manners. You needed to be able to take part in dinner-table conversation (which in those days was considered an art form), and, naturally, you needed to be able to appreciate what you were eating.

But that was then, and this is now. Even people who work at home (like me) are hard-pressed. To get the house cleaned up, and arrange the meals and make sure the recorder gets practiced and homework done, to supervise the millions of things for which children need supervision, and pay the bills and register to vote, and to have a few seconds for friendship or to read a book and then to shop and cook and plan menus! Wouldn't it be easier if we threw up our hands, ate junk food, and ordered out?

It would probably be easier, but it would be far less nice. These days family life (or private life) is a challenge, and we must all fight for it. We must turn off the television and the telephone, hunker down in front of our hearths, and leave our briefcases at the office, if for only one night. We must march into the kitchen, en famille or with a friend, and find some easy, heartwarming things to make from scratch, and even if it is but once a week, we must gather at the table, alone or with friends or with lots of friends or with one friend, and eat a meal together. We know that without food we would die. Without fellowship life is not worth living.

For every overworked professional woman of the nineties

there was a depressed, bored, nonworking housewife of the fifties. We cannot go back in time. Instead, we must reinvent life for ourselves.

The table is a meeting place, a gathering ground, the source of sustenance and nourishment, festivity, safety, and satisfaction. A person cooking is a person giving: Even the simplest food is a gift.

My goal has been to find recipes that are easy, fast, and delicious that can be served to a family of three or for a large feast. I know that young children will wander away from the table, and that family life is never smooth, and that life itself is full, not only of charm and warmth and comfort but of sorrow and tears. But whether we are happy or sad, we must be fed. Both happy and sad people can be cheered up by a nice meal. This book was written for the sustainers and those who will be sustained. I hope both will eat happily and well from it.

Laurie Colwin
New York City, 1992

Why I Love Cookbooks

When I was a little girl my mother became a fund-raiser. She was terrific at this, and she used to go to very rich people's houses for dinner, and the next morning I would say, "What was it like?" On one occasion she went to a huge fund-raising party at the home of the mushroom king of Kennett Square, Pennsylvania, where all of our white button mushrooms grow. I made her tell me this story about seven hundred thousand times because—and this is probably why I am a writer—there was not one detail that my mother, who is a kind of variant form of Hollywood reporter, did not remember. She remembered that the plates had been specially made by Limoges and they had mushrooms on them. She remembered that the first course was a mushroom salad, and the second course was a mushroom bouillon, and the third course was a filet of beef with . . . mushrooms. Something else happened, I can't remember what it was, probably a mushroom sorbet—and then they had green spun sugar, and in the middle of the green spun sugar were little fondant mushrooms dipped in chocolate and then rubbed in cocoa on the top so they would look just like *boleti*.

Like my mother, I like to know what everybody ate. My

friends are constantly driven crazy by me because I want to know what they had for dinner. I want to know what they had and how they cooked it. I'm not very curious about what people had *out*. I'm interested in what people have *in,* because I'm very interested in people's domestic lives. I used to think I was frittering away my time, but the fact is, what is more interesting than how people live? I personally can't think of anything. Maybe war, or death or something, but not to me. I like to know how they serve food, what they do with it, how it looks.

I was at a cocktail party not too long ago, and someone started to talk to me about *Anna Karenina,* and whoever this person was filled me with such a blinding desire to read this book that I felt that I had to get out of there at once and find a copy and read it. Well, fortunately, they had one on the shelf. So I said, "Excuse me, could I borrow this book?" They said, "Sure." I said, "Bye!" and I left. And as I was reading *Anna Karenina,* I discovered an amazing thing. The food in that book is really *great.* There's a dinner that Levin has with some other guy, and *everything is described.* When you read it at two o'clock in the morning, and it's cold out, and you're in bed, all you want to do is go out and have that meal.

Basically, all I ever do is read. I read about monastic life, polar Eskimos, arctic travel—I have no interest in ever going to the Arctic, by the way, and as I am not Christian, I can never enter a monastery—and I read English novels. One of my favorite novelists is Barbara Pym, who is an underrated writer, like Jane Austen. Everybody thinks she's just darling, but she is not just darling, she's really tough. One of the great things about Barbara Pym is that the food in Barbara Pym is *just wonderful.*

I realize the reason I love cookbooks is that cookbooks leave out all the other stuff. You don't have to find out about family relationships. It's just like Barbara Pym, but there's no novel! It's just the food.

I never really read cookbooks until I was about twenty-four. I worked in publishing, in a division of Random House that I will not name, but because I worked in a division of Random House I could order any Random House, Pantheon, or Knopf book I wanted. Someone said, "Why don't you order that nice book *Italian Food* by Elizabeth David?" And I said, "Oh, sure, I'll do that," and I did. I have it in hardcover, and it has little roach specks on the top.

I had an English boss who was very petite, and he was going back to England. He and his wife invited me to their good-bye party, and at their good-bye party I behaved so badly that even for me it was really bad, and I got toweringly drunk, and I was sick all the way down Broadway—I lived in Greenwich Village, and this party was at Columbia University, and for those of you who don't know New York, that's a really far piece.

The next day I woke up and felt as if someone had run over me with a semi. I was in terrible shape. But because I was twenty-four, and twenty-four-year-olds don't stay sick as long as older people, I found that by the time it was eleven o'clock and I had slept all morning and drunk a lot of lime juice and seltzer water, which is my personal cure for this sort of thing, I felt that I should read something, and I happened to light on my copy of *Italian Food*, by Elizabeth David, which I had never read. I spent the afternoon recovering from this massive hangover and reading *Italian Food*. By the time it was dinnertime, I was so hungry I was about to eat my pillow. My friend from this unnamed division of Random House appeared at my door bearing two little veal medallions, some watercress, and I can't remember what else. I stood up—I was amazed that I could do that—and I cooked dinner. It was probably the best meal I've ever had in my entire life. It started to dawn on me that there was something about reading cookbooks that was extremely attractive. Then I read some of them when I was sober and found that they had the same effect on me.

Cookbooks hit you where you live. You want comfort; you want security; you want food; you want to not be hungry; and not only do you want those basic things fixed, you want it done in a really nice, gentle way that makes you feel loved. That's a big desire, and cookbooks say to the person who's reading them, "If you will read me, you will be able to do this for yourself and for others. You will make everybody feel better."

There are many cookbooks by my bedside, with all the little pages turned down. If somebody pressed me to the wall and asked me to justify myself, I would have to say that it is very true that there is nothing like a cookbook to explain to you how we used to live. If you want to know what *real* life used to be like, meaning domestic life, there isn't anywhere you can go that gives you a better idea than a cookbook.

And for those of you who are suffering from sadness or hangover, or are feeling blue or tired of life, if you're not going to read *Persuasion*, you may as well read *Italian Food* by Elizabeth David.

Adapted from a talk given to the Radcliffe Culinary Friends,
May 17, 1992

After the Holidays

There are those of us—the harried, cowardly, overextended—who find the beginning of December to be life's most trying time. The holidays are upon us. All over America, frantic people (mostly women, it seems to me) are trying to cope with the endless list of things to do or buy, wrap, and take to the post office. There are all sorts of tasks—shopping, baking, errand running, and gifts forgotten that must be bought at the last minute. These winter decathloners often have jobs and children, too.

Then come the holidays themselves, like an exploding rocket, leaving wrapping paper everywhere, to say nothing of the remains of the elegant meal, tired and overfed guests, and exhausted hosts. And one day later it is all over and life is back to normal.

I myself long for New Year's Eve, a perfect night to stay home with a couple of similarly New Year's Eve–phobic close friends. A nice simple meal, a fire if it's cold outside. The holidays are behind me, and I can relax, cheerful with the thought that the big deal is just a memory.

I have made the same dinner for New Year's Eve for ages. I serve biscuits and marinated Brussels sprouts along with some grilled fish, usually salmon. For dessert, I have lemon rice pudding. My New Year's Eve meal is meant to be relaxing for both cook and guests, a trustworthy dinner that does not take up much time.

First come the Brussels sprouts, which can be made in advance. Some people love them and others dread them, but lots of fence sitters on the issue are swayed by this slightly unexpected first course. It is my attempt to reproduce the Cajun-style sprouts of a now-departed restaurant, La Louisiana.

Marinated Brussels Sprouts

Slice the Brussels sprouts in half and steam them until tender. Then mix up any marinade you want. For 1 pound of sprouts I use ¾ cup olive oil, ¾ cup lemon juice, cayenne to taste, 1 teaspoon celery salt, a crushed clove of garlic, and a dash of Angostura bitters. But the variations on the seasoning are endless: a little spike of ground cloves, a sprinkle of Worcestershire or Pickapeppa sauce, or balsamic or garlic vinegar. I cover the sprouts with the dressing while they are still warm, then store them in the fridge overnight or all day, and serve them with *arugula* at room temperature. A few toasted walnuts scattered around add a festive touch.

As for the fish, I like salmon. Norwegian salmon is good and smooth, but if your fish store ever has the Pacific Coast variety, go for it. Pacific Coast salmon is redder and firmer, its texture slightly drier, and its flavor far more intense. A fillet of fish is a cook's best friend.

Broiled Salmon

Simply paint the skinless side of the fillet with *tamari* (a Japanese soy sauce) or regular soy sauce, stick the fish under the broiler (about 6 inches from the heat) for about 15 minutes, and you will never look back. You can serve this with dill sauce or with an assortment of Indian condiments: chutney, hot lime pickle, and spicy *raita* (yogurt with cucumbers and such things as coriander or cayenne). I usually throw together a *salsa* by chopping up 1 green bell pepper, 2 scallions, a fresh *jalapeño,* a couple of best-quality canned tomatoes (½ cup), and a large garlic clove and adding 3 tablespoons fresh lime juice, 2 tablespoons olive oil, and maybe a dash of salt.

If you are just the tiniest bit energetic, it does not take too much effort to make plain, old-fashioned baking powder biscuits. It is my impression that no one bakes these anymore—at least not from scratch—because when I produce them people fall on them. I add Parmesan cheese, or grated Cheddar, and a little pepper or toasted sesame seeds. You can put in anything you like—the basic procedure is the same. This recipe is a combination of one in *Charleston Receipts* and another from Elizabeth David's *Spices, Salt and Aromatics in the English Kitchen.*

Parmesan Sesame Biscuits

1. Sift 2 cups flour with 1 tablespoon baking powder and ¼ teaspoon cayenne.

2. Cut or rub in 2 tablespoons butter.

3. Add 1½ cups grated Parmesan (or Cheddar) and 1 tablespoon lightly toasted sesame seeds (let them cool first).

4. Add about 1¼ cups buttermilk (or a combination of milk and yogurt) and stir until the mixture forms a dough. Knead 6 times on a floured board.

5. Roll out to about ½ inch and cut with a round cutter (a plain drinking glass or cookie cutter will do just fine). When I use a 2¼-inch cutter, I get 20 biscuits.

6. Arrange on a baking sheet and bake at 425° F. for 12 to 15 minutes.

I have kind of a crush on biscuit cutters, and when I see them at flea markets I always buy them. I have little ones, big ones, ones with scalloped edges, and some in the shape of hearts, clubs, diamonds, and spades, doubtless for some long-ago ladies' bridge lunch. You can make these biscuits big and flat or small and puffy like mini dinner rolls. It doesn't matter: They are always wonderful.

And now for the rice pudding, neglected nursery staple. Ending New Year's Eve on this sort of childlike note appeals to me. Rice pudding—creamy and consoling—is, in my opinion, just the thing to set you up for the year ahead. I like this rice pudding, from Jane Grigson's *Good Things* (but then I like practically everything in Jane Grigson's *Good Things*).

Lemon Rice Pudding

1. Wash ¼ cup rice (I have used Arborio and *basmati*, and jasmine. Arborio makes this pudding a bit too thick).

2. With a vegetable peeler take off strips about ¼ inch wide from 1 lemon. I chop these up fine, although the original recipe leaves them whole.

3. Put the rice, the lemon zest, 1½ tablespoons sugar, and 1 pint of half-and-half into a flameproof dish. Cook in a very slow oven (250° F.) for 2½ hours, stirring every 45 minutes. Then add the juice of 1 lemon.

4. If the pudding is too solid, add some cream or more half-and-half. Chill the pudding very well. Mrs. Grigson suggests adding cinnamon toward the end of the cooking, but I don't like it in my rice pudding, so, when it's done, I sprinkle the top with brown sugar and run it under the broiler as for *crème brûlée*.

Mrs. Grigson says: "You will find that the lemon peel has almost dissolved, and so has the rice, although it still feels gently grainy to the tongue."

Your New Year's Eve dinner is almost ready, as you have made the rice pudding, the *salsa* for the salmon, and the Brussels sprouts early in the day or the night before. The fish takes hardly any time, and then you only need some plain small potatoes and blanched asparagus and you're in business. The biscuits, which can be made in advance and reheated but are perfect straight out of the oven, are totally optional. They may seem like too much work unless your New Year's Eve day, like mine, includes a child on school vacation who is happy to sit around the house on a cold day—and help make biscuits—so long as she and her mother get to split half a pound of smoked salmon (an expensive touch that now amounts to a ritual). But even if you have no help at all, this is an easy dinner, one a person can be proud to serve.

But what if you feel it is *too* simple? For the ambitious (and the rest of us who like to do something special once in a while) the answer is *tuiles*. These fragile almond cookies get taken off the baking sheet and hung over a rolling pin to cool so that they resemble (or are meant to resemble) French roofing tiles. This recipe comes from Margaret Costa's *The Four Seasons' Cookery Book*.

Almond Tuiles

1. Cream 5 tablespoons softened butter with ¼ cup sugar. Stir in ⅓ cup flour and ⅓ cup sliced or chopped almonds (a big knife and a cutting board are all you need).

2. Form the mixture into a dough (you may need to add a very little bit of milk).

3. Drop by teaspoons a few inches apart onto a baking sheet lined with parchment paper and flatten the cookies with a fork dipped in cold water. Do not bake too many at one time: These cookies spread.

4. Bake at 400° F. for 6 to 8 minutes, or until brown on the edges. Let cool for 1 or 2 minutes, and then lift gently with a spatula and drape over a rolling pin to cool. You'll have about 26 *tuiles*.

Happy New Year!

Black Beans

I had my first taste of black bean soup on a cold winter Saturday when I was sixteen years old. A friend, home for the holidays from a very glamorous college, gave a lunch party and invited me. Seated at her table, I felt that I—mired in high school and barely passing geometry—had died and entered a heaven in which people played the cello, stayed up at night discussing Virginia Woolf, saw plays by Jean-Paul Sartre, and went to Paris for their junior years abroad. But it was the black bean soup that changed my life.

It came straight out of a can and was spiked with Sherry and served in bisque cups with thin, round slices of lemon. It seemed to me homey and exotic at the same time, and I have loved it ever since. Of all canned soups, black bean is still the only one that tastes okay to me, but then I have never had a black bean soup I didn't like.

It is hard not to dote on black beans (which are also known as turtle beans). They make magnificent soups, puréed or lumpy. They are the basis for innumerable one-pot meals, such as rice and beans and *feijoada* (a Brazilian black bean and sausage stew). Paired with little red beans, they make a noble chili, with or without meat.

Black beans are the frazzled person's friend. They are easy to fix, high in protein and fiber, valued as a cholesterol buster, and useful in hundreds of dishes. Most encouragingly, they are one of the few things you can serve from a can without cringing. A home without canned black beans—or chick-peas or *cannellini* beans, for that matter—is a house that is *not stocked for an emergency*. A can of black beans will get a hungry person out of trouble.

For soups, however, the dried beans are best. Combined with stock, garlic, hot red pepper flakes, onions, and tomatoes, black beans make a delicious, stewy soup that you can serve to your down-to-earth friends with a bowl of rice and a big bottle of hot sauce. Or you can add a cup of red wine and some *kielbasa* or *chorizo* or both, and, with a pan of corn bread, feed it all to a party. You can make black bean soup with all kinds of vegetables or with almost nothing in it but the beans. No matter what you do, black beans will never let you down.

The Chinese are well aware of this. They sweeten black beans and stick them in pastries. They also ferment them and cook them with shrimp. Since the first time I tasted a fermented black bean, I have never been without a supply. (If you live near a Chinatown, you can buy them there in large bags. Otherwise, some supermarkets have them in jars, and many Chinese cookbooks provide lists of mail-order sources for exotic ingredients.) It is amazing what fermented beans find their way into: *ratatouille*, pasta with eggplant, sautéed green beans. Oh, the black bean is a wonderful thing!

On the fancy end, a black bean, crab, and corn salad is hard to beat. For those who don't eat seafood, a salad of black beans, sun-dried tomatoes, and avocados is award-winning, too. In fact, it's hard to find something (other than, say, poached pears) with which black beans aren't nice. They cozy up divinely to corn, tomatoes, butternut squash, and even potatoes, a curious-sounding yet very yummy match.

But for people who are lazy, tired, or just plain rushed, black bean soup is the big winner, hands down. You can make it in your sleep. It can literally be made *while* you sleep. I am a great fan of things that cook while you dream or work. When my daughter was a tot, we lived on black bean soup. In fact, we still do. My recipe for it is a sort of dirty little secret, because it is so *convenient.*

I would like to be able to say that I make my own stock and freeze it, but I don't. My freezer is about the size of a first-class postage stamp, and therefore I have no room. I also have no time. I am not terribly ashamed to reveal that I use canned broth, most often the low-salt variety. Canned broth is usually pretty awful and should *never* be used in anything in which its flavor is paramount. If you are going to have *tortellini in brodo,* make your own stock—or eat out—is my advice.

For Black Bean Soup, however, beef broth from a can is fine. Soak 2 cups of dried beans in cold water to cover for 1 hour and drain them. Combine them in a large pot with two 12-ounce cans of beef broth and one 28-ounce can of peeled tomatoes. People in a hurry often open the can, drain the juice into the pot, and then slice up the tomatoes with a knife while they are still in the can. I would never let anyone catch me doing this, but I do it all the time. Add 1 cup of water, 2 big cloves of garlic, chopped up fine, 1 minced onion, and 2 or 3 smallish potatoes, cut into pieces.

Cover the pot, put it on a flame tamer over very low heat, and get lost. (I am on record in my belief that the flame tamer—a widely available metal disk that reduces a flame's intensity—can be the source of much domestic tranquility, but it *is* a somewhat controversial piece of equipment, because many people would never dream of leaving the house with the stove on. I, however, do it all the time.)

On a flame tamer, a good black bean soup takes at least 5 hours to cook, hours in which you could be writing a novel, composing a brief, arguing with your dry cleaner, or playing catch with your child and her friends. You might yak on the telephone, balance your checkbook, or go through piles of work. You might even go shopping for yourself, remembering to stop afterward to buy some bread and cheese. But whatever you do, while your soup is cooking, *you are not*.

Once the 5 hours are up, stir in the juice of 1 lime. Then you can decide what texture you want your soup to have. You can purée part of it in the blender and then stir the purée back into the rest of the soup. You can purée the whole thing in batches in the blender with some yogurt or buttermilk. Or you can leave the soup alone. And then, because black beans are kind and friendly, you can either have a hot black bean soup if the weather is cold or, if it's warm out, you can have a heavenly cold black bean soup with a dollop of yogurt or sour cream and a dash of cumin on top.

Should friends call at the last minute and say they are coming by, you might—if you are truly unhinged—make an evening of it. After the soup, you could open a can of black beans and serve them as a second course with a vinaigrette, or you could toss plain old spaghetti with olive oil, garlic, hot red pepper flakes, and fermented black beans. For dessert you could buy a few Chinese moon cakes, those flat, flaky cakes filled with red beans or winter melon. They have a red double happiness symbol stamped on them, and, if you happen to be *obsessed*, they are also made with a sweet paste of . . . black beans.

Lemons and Limes

If I were forced to give up every fruit in the world but one I would have absolutely no trouble choosing. The lemon wins, hands down.

The lemon is the workhorse of the food world: dependable, versatile, and available all year round. You can preserve it in salt, as the Moroccans do, and stuff your chicken with it, or you can stick it into a suet crust surrounded by butter, as the British do. You can dice it up and put it into a salad with red onion and Italian parsley. You can make lemon cookies, lemon cake, lemon icing, lemonade (hot or cold), lemon flip, and lemon rice pudding. A drop of lemon juice and a strip of lemon peel make a chicken soup divine. A tablespoon of lemon juice in your pesto brings all the flavors together. People who find vinegar hard to take love lemon juice in their salad dressing, and people on low- or no-salt diets find lemon juice just the thing. The ascorbic acid it contains makes things taste salty.

There are even people who eat lemons out of hand. I myself have been eating lemons since a child. By rights I should have no enamel left on my teeth. Considering that on a cold weekend in

England when I was twenty-two I ate an entire bag of them, it is a wonder I have any teeth at all.

I don't think I have ever been without a supply of lemons in my kitchen since I started cooking. As a mere youth, I used to make large crocks of something we all called Chinese Ginger Cabbage. You cut up a green cabbage as for coleslaw, salt it liberally, dress it with dark sesame oil, sprinkle it with powdered ginger, and squirt over it the juice of a lemon or two. Toss and weigh down with a plate. I ate large quantities of this stuff. On the one hand it is terrible for you (all that salt); on the other, it is wonderful for you (all that cabbage). I never make it anymore because it is too salty, but in those days I had no oven, whereas nowadays, I do, and therefore I can roast a chicken anytime I want, and I never roast a chicken without stuffing it with half a lemon.

Half a lemon in a chicken is a wonderful thing. Since I never season chicken with salt, lemon gives a salty taste. When you spill the juices from the chicken cavity into the roasting pan to make pan juice, they come out lemony. Lemon and chicken are a wondrous marriage. There are even people who like to sprinkle their fried chicken with a little lemon juice.

Of course there is no fish course without lemon. Fish and lemon are made for each other, and if you marinate raw flounder in lemon (or lime) juice with hot peppers, you get *ceviche*. It is impossible to make tuna fish salad (at least in this house) without lemon juice, and a few drops on top of grilled salmon is the perfect touch. Then, should you have any cold salmon left over, a drop of mayonnaise, some chopped scallion, and lemon juice make the perfect salmon salad.

Lemon and beef are not the ideal couple, except when it comes to marinating. Any good marinade has a little lemon juice in it, and the day after a dinner party, with a bit of flank steak left over, nothing is nicer than cold beef salad: sliced beef, hot pepper flakes, scallions, parsley, olive oil, and lemon juice. If you serve this with cold, dressed lentils, you actually have another meal. And what to dress the lentils with? Olive oil, black pepper, salt, and lemon juice, with a big clove of garlic smashed in.

And now to dessert. Here is the lemon's shining moment. Lemon ice, lemon pound cake, and lemon pudding cake. Lemon squares, bars, and shortcake. Lemon fluff, Madeira cake (with lemon in it), lemon jelly, plain lemon cookies. Besides chocolate, the longest entry in many cookbook indexes is for lemons. I adore a recipe from Jane Grigson's *Good Things*. New Year's Eve I try out her lemon rice pudding (see "After the Holidays"), which you make with cream (or half-and-half), rice, sugar, and lemon peel. You bake it slowly in the oven, adding a drop or two of lemon juice, and stir it up from the bottom from time to time. The resulting pudding, served very cold with a couple of blanched pistachio nuts, will make rice pudding lovers crumble into bits. The rice almost dissolves on the tongue, but is not mushy. It is suave, sophisticated baby food with a wonderful lemon taste. The tiny pieces of peel have been cooked to a candy. This dessert is innocent and wicked at the same time, the ideal end to a dinner welcoming in a new year.

When there are no good-looking lemons, I buy limes. Both should be thin skinned, for the thicker the skin, the drier the fruit. If a lemon looks puffy and feels light, it probably hasn't much juice, although a thick-skinned lemon is useful if what you want is zest.

A hard lime is often difficult to squeeze, whereas one with a little more give will yield more juice. Although their taste is completely different, I use lemons and limes interchangeably. A chicken stuffed with a lime is delicious and tastes of lime. The same goes for cookies and bars and shortbread. Lime shortbread is refreshingly exotic but only slightly so. There are those who say that what we get up north are not limes. Limes from the Florida Keys are limes, not those little green handballs found around town. I will confess I have never tasted a key lime, or a Meyer lemon, for that matter. I know I am the poorer for it. I have had key lime pie made with up-north limes, and I have made Meyer lemon tart from a recipe of Alice Waters using plain old lemons. Both were remarkably good and are probably even more remarkable if you have the real thing.

But until the real thing comes along, I am happy with the limes and lemons I can get anywhere.

And when you have run out of things to cook with lemons, you can use them as medicine. When you or a loved one is sick with the flu, a very good remedy is

Hot Lemonade

For this you need one big water glass. Into the bottom of it put 1 large spoonful of honey and 1 cinnamon stick. Slice half a lemon into thin slices and put those in, too. Now squeeze the remaining lemon half, and 1 more lemon, and put the juice of both into the glass. Fill with hot water, stir, and serve to the sick person with the glass wrapped in a napkin.

While the sick person is recovering you can tidy up the house using a bottle of lemon oil furniture polish, and when you are finished you can sit and have a cup of Lemon Zinger tea and a lovely little snack: lemon and poppy seed biscuits and some little Niçoise olives flavored with lemon zest.

The Once and Future Dinner Party

Once upon a time, not so long ago, giving a dinner party was a snap. A filet of beef, a leg of lamb, roast duck. A couple of inconsequential vegetables, a salad of some sort or another, and for dessert something fancy. Nowadays a menu like that makes some people envision little skulls and crossbones of the sort that used to be put on bottles of poison.

In the past three decades many things we counted on are said to have fallen by the wayside: the corner grocery store, the sweet shoppe that served egg creams, the nuclear family. These things, of course, can still be found. What cannot be found is a group of people who will sit down and eat what you feed them without problem. And what cannot be reclaimed is that happy, mindless sense of festive occasion in which no one thought it odd if your dinner party consisted of a rib roast with a crackling rim of fat, a runny triple cream cheese with the salad, garlic bread, blue cheese dressing, and a dessert made with a pint or two of cream and six egg yolks. How did we ever, ever eat that way? And how will we ever manage now when half one's pals are on diets, the other half have food allergies, and the third half, so to speak, simply will not and cannot bear to eat that way anymore.

These old-fashioned dinner parties may be given, but not by me. I spend my nights sleepless and tossing while trying to figure out how to give a dinner party with no fat in it. If cream and butter were once the hostess's best friends, where is she to find her new best friends?

I have given this considerable thought since the night two years ago when I was called upon to make a birthday dinner for my cousin Joe.

My cousin Joe is a real estate baron, and while in many ways he is just like a normal person, he is fanatical about his diet. His idea of a swell vacation is to put in time at the Pritikin Institute clocking his cholesterol levels. This dinner party presented a formidable challenge, since in addition to being fanatic he has a sensitive palate. Besides, his wife, Aimee, was pregnant, and I felt called upon to feed her something delicious.

Having produced a meal that seemed a howling success, I have come to realize that the hostess's new best friends are no-fat yogurt and puréed beans. If this sounds dreary I assure you it is not.

The first course of this birthday meal was Cold Yogurt Soup, the easiest soup in the world to make and good at any time of the year: no-fat yogurt, defatted chicken stock, skinned cucumbers, a pinch of cumin, and the juice of half a lemon. There are endless variations on this theme: the addition of cooked grated beets, a teaspoon of curry, a small clove of garlic. The blender does all the work for you. The soup is put in the fridge and forgotten until dinnertime, when it is garnished with chopped parsley, chopped dill, scallions, chives, or all of them.

The second course—a little courselette, really—was a palate teaser of Spicy Brussels Sprouts.

A fat-free main course presents many challenges to the average dinner-party giver, but wonderful ideas can be found in Italian cookbooks. I went searching through the collected works of Marcella Hazan, who is a constant inspiration, and found a very attractive recipe for a Purée of Cranberry Beans in a Béchamel Sauce. With a few adjustments, this recipe did the trick.

Cranberry beans, dried or fresh, are milky white and mottled with pinkish red. For this dish they are cooked with fresh sage (or a bay leaf) and a few cloves of garlic. When they are almost tender, a peeled potato is cooked along with them. The beans are strained, the liquid reserved, and the beans pushed through a sieve or food mill. The resulting purée is meant to be tipped into a classic béchamel sauce (butter, flour, and milk), but a perfectly fine substitute is a sauce made of oil, flour, and a combination of bean liquid and low-fat milk. The purée can be eaten as is or spooned into an attractive oiled dish, scattered with 1 tablespoon of Parmesan cheese (or seasoned bread crumbs), and run under the broiler to crisp up on top.

With this I served a platter of naked asparagus, another of sliced cucumbers (dressing on the side), and baked potatoes (not my idea, but requested by my cousin).

A small green salad followed, and for dessert we had fruit salad. For those who feel that fruit salad is not enough, it can always be served with sherbet and meringues.

The interesting thing about this dinner was how *keen* I felt the next morning—light as a feather and ready to fly. It probably set me up for the magnificently killing dinner party that followed several weeks later.

We were invited to a midwinter party by a terrific cook who wanted to serve something warm and cheering.

When we got to his house he was in the kitchen whipping up the mashed potatoes. I watched him pour the hot milk and pounds of butter into them. This mountain of potatoes was put in the middle of a hot platter and surrounded by *boudins blancs et noirs* (or black and white sausages). The *blancs* are made with veal and cream. The *noirs* are made with pig's blood. I can't think of anything worse for you than black sausage (or blood pudding as they are sometimes called). But once every thirty years they are really quite irresistible.

The pièce de résistance was a bowl of big, fat cloves of garlic that had been blanched in milk and then caramelized in butter and brown sugar. To this day it embarrasses me to remember how I disgraced myself with these. You were supposed to make a little dent in your potatoes and ladle in a discreet (not in my case) portion of garlic. I also seem to remember through a haze of garlic cloves a green salad and an orange cake. The next morning my little daughter hugged me and then sniffed in wonderment. "Mommy," she said. "Your *arms* smell of garlic!"

It is hard to describe how terrible I felt that morning. I am not much of a drinker: My limit is one beer. I was hung over from the food. I felt bottom heavy, like Baby Huey. As the day wore on and I began to feel more like a person and less like an old chewed slipper I reflected on these two dinner parties, the lean and the fat. In the old days, anything went. How your guests felt the next morning was their affair. People chowed down their beef Wellington and leg of lamb and potatoes scalloped in cream, and no one in polite society uttered the word *triglyceride*—in the old days, of course, no one in *any* society knew about these things.

But now not only does a hostess have to find a bunch of compatible people who might like to spend a few hours together, she is responsible for their health and welfare, too. She has to know which oil is monounsaturated or poly, and which fish will scatter your lipids and what lipids are the right or wrong ones. The modern cook stands in the kitchen with cookbook in one hand and *The New England Journal of Medicine* in the other.

My future is clear before me. I am going to sit around trying to figure out delicious and interesting things to feed people that are actually *good* for them. And once or twice a year I will be invited to one of those dinner parties of the past, come home, recover, and plan more menus for the dinner parties of the future.

The Duck Dilemma

Every once in a while, even the most sensible person gets a craving for roast duck. Some people are more efficient than others: Those who happen to be organized and lucky enough to live near a Chinatown purchase one of those mahogany-colored glazed ducks hanging from a hook in shop windows.

Or you might call up your significant other and take him or her out for Peking duck at a place that does not require reserving your duck in advance. Or you might get in touch with the one person you know with a duck press, which looks like a guillotine combined with a mangle washer in the shape of a giant corkscrew. Of course, it is hard to find a pal who has a duck press. Pressed duck (which is duck breast and skin pressed into a convenient little shape and then roasted—or roasted and then pressed; I never remember the order) used to be on the menus of old-fashioned French restaurants and has now gone the way of the black-and-white television set and the bouffant hairdo.

These days duck is often served rare. I myself cannot imagine why anyone would want to eat rare duck—which, like rare lamb, is in my opinion an abomination. People who like this sort of thing should order *Carpaccio* and leave the poor duck alone.

Let us assume that you have not made it to Chinatown, and your sweetie does not want to go out for Peking duck, and furthermore your friend with the duck press sold it only last week to an antiques dealer for several thousand dollars.

If you are going to have Roast Duck, you are going to have to do it yourself, which is time-consuming but not complicated. A duck is easy enough to find. If your butcher does not have a fresh one, a frozen one is all right, too. Duck is something that freezes really well. If you buy a fresh duck in Chinatown you have to contend with the feet and head—a disconcerting sight. It is best to deal with these issues when small children are not in the kitchen with you. Save the feet for duck soup.

To begin, pull all the extraneous fat out of the cavity and set it aside. Those people with extremely low cholesterol levels can make *grieben*, the Jewish crackling, by rendering the diced-up duck fat and frying chopped onions in it. These delicious and extremely unhealthy morsels can be scattered on top of vegetables or incorporated into a *focaccia* or used to garnish a timbale of polenta.

Stuff the duck with an orange, cut in half, and a few big, smashed garlic cloves. Then, with a very sharp little fork, pierce the skin all over; this lets the fat out during roasting. Season the duck with paprika and black pepper, pop it on a rack, and slide it into a hot oven—400° F. is about right.

Your duck will weigh 5 to 6 pounds, and for the first hour of cooking you will swear that at least 3 of these pounds are fat. You must constantly remove this from the pan. Woe to the beginner who forgets this, inviting the possibility of a fire and filling the

kitchen and the rest of the house with the terrible smell of burn-
ing fat.

You can keep the duck fat, as the French do, to fry your potatoes in, or give it to friends who like their potatoes lethal, or
discard it in some ecologically responsible way (never down the
drain!).

After an hour, turn the oven heat down to 325° F. and roast
your duck for another hour, removing all the fat you can with a
bulb baster or soup spoon. When it looks as if the fat has all melted
and the duck juices begin to flow, it is time to start basting. Some
people squeeze lemon or lime on top of the duck at this point.
Others prefer orange juice. All these things are delicious, but the
sweetness of orange is a natural with the slight gaminess of duck.

Continue cooking your duck, and basting it, for another hour.
I like to roast a duck until the meat falls off the bones and the skin
is very crisp and succulent. This is not everyone's cup of tea, so to
speak, and cooking times can be changed to accommodate those
who like their duck a little less tender. A roasted duck can stay
happily in a warm oven without drying out; the layer of crisp skin
keeps it moist.

Because most people only eat duck once in a while, it is
probably right to make something of an occasion of it. I always
think I am going to break down and buy some of those frilly paper pantaloons you get in cookware stores and put them on the
duck legs. (These are a sure hit with small children, who like to
put them on their fingers.) But I have never gotten around to it.
However, I cannot serve duck without thinking of the immortal
R. Crumb, the genius of comic-book art, incomparable master
of Head Comix, and creator of the magnificent strip "Ducks Yas
Yas," which illustrates the following deeply felt poem:

Mama bought a rooster
Thought it was a duck
Brought it to the table
With its legs straight up

And now that your duck is roasting, what to serve with it? You want something plain or rather acidic. A steamed vegetable with a drop of lemon juice is nice, and so is puréed butternut squash. Remember that the duck is the centerpiece: A little bite is very rich and makes everyone feel full. Things like corn bread, spoon bread, and polenta go well with duck as long as there is not too much of them.

After duck a salad is a necessity. The ideal dish is the beautiful Composed Salad described in a book titled *Kitchen in Corfu,* by James Chatto and W. L. Martin (New Amsterdam Books). Slice 1 big, sweet onion into rounds. On top of each round place a slice of peeled orange. On top of that scatter some chopped green olives, a little cracked black pepper, a dash of olive oil, and perhaps a drop or two of lemon juice. This exotic salad is as refreshing as it is attractive and can be produced almost year round. Its sharpness and saltiness contrast with the buttery luxuriousness of the duck. In addition to being very simple to put together, it is very, very delicious.

Now you have had your duck and salad and perhaps a small dish of fruit for dessert. So what do you do with the leftover duck?

Take the meat off the carcass and put it in a kettle. Add the feet, if you have them, and all the bones. Add 2 smashed garlic cloves, enough water to cover, and gently simmer everything for about 6 hours. Strain it all into a jar (you should have about 4 cups); put the jar, uncovered, in the fridge; and, when the stock cools down, take the fat off the top and make Pepper Soup.

Take 2 small, cut-up red bell peppers, 1 (or more) hottish pepper, a tablespoon of paprika, a pinch of salt, and the duck stock and gently simmer this for an hour or so. Then either strain the soup immediately, merely pressing the peppers against the sieve for a consommé, or purée the soup first, then strain it, for a kind of bisque.

As for the leftover duck meat, if you happen to have any, you can try to replicate, as have I, the wonderful green pasta with spicy duck sauce that used to be served at the now-defunct but still lamented Tenth Avenue Bar in Manhattan. I have never been able to get this quite right, but the idea is to make a sauce of garlic, tiny Niçoise olives, a little chicken stock, Pickapeppa sauce (you can buy this at the supermarket), lemon juice, and shredded duck meat.

This sauce is rather like the Lost Chord. I cannot give a recipe because I don't have one. All I have is those ingredients, which can be fiddled with. Even if you have never tasted the original, what you get when you mess around with these components is always good.

Or have your duck cold on a bed of cucumbers or as a sandwich with *arugula* on sourdough bread. Whichever way you have it, once a year, duck is wonderful—yas yas.

Boiled Beef

I am not a vegetarian, although I have spates of vegetarianism and there are times when a strictly vegetarian diet is my goal. But at other times, particularly when it is cold and rainy outside, what I want is boiled beef. I produce this dish twice a year, usually when meat-eating company is coming for dinner.

There are endless variations on this theme, and recipes—including *pot-au-feu, flanken,* and New England boiled dinner—abound from everywhere. They all come down to the same thing: some beef, some vegetables, something aromatic, and water.

The best boiled beef I ever ate was at the Ukrainian Restaurant in the Ukrainian National Home on the Lower East Side of Manhattan. I would gladly go out in a violent storm and walk over broken glass to have some. It was rich and savory and tasted like essence of prime rib—how they did it I cannot imagine.

The second best was at Luchow's, the late lamented German restaurant, a place with old wood paneling, old waiters, Blue Willow plates, and lots of older people speaking German. The restaurant served boiled beef in aspic. And, furthermore, it had been turned into a work of art. A slice of beef, two carrots sliced on the diagonal, two perfect rounds of onion, all beautifully arranged under a sheet of amber aspic—a lovely dish.

My boiled beef looks nothing like this, but then I am not a restaurant chef. It is very unlikely that I will ever create an amber aspic, and even if I did I do not think I could get anyone I know to eat it. The world, as we know, divides unequally between those who love aspic (not too many) and those who loathe and fear it (most).

My boiled beef does not pledge allegiance to any particular ethnic group. Rather it is a kind of free-lance association of this and that from many recipes.

First, there is the issue of the beef. Many people feel that proper boiled beef calls for brisket, and these people have a lot going for them. I, however, feel that if you are going to plunk down your child's future college money for brisket there are other things to do with this cut. Besides, brisket is too *fancy* for such a humble dish.

I have had many conversations with butchers on this subject, and I have tried different cuts. Rump, for instance, is nice but fibrous. And chuck is yummy but fatty. My personal favorite happens to be bottom round, which has the virtues of being succulent and full of flavor.

Most recipes encourage you to put in a split calf's foot, and most recipes are right. But in these modern times a calf's foot is not the easiest thing to find. Some veal bones will do nicely enough. It goes without saying that if you can get your hands on organic meat you should grab it and run. Organic beef is leaner and tastier than almost anything you can get in a supermarket, although you can now buy a type called "specialty beef." This is usually grass-fed, slaughtered young, and tested for hormones and pesticides. This beef is very tender, quick-cooking, and also extremely delicious as well as more expensive. But if you don't eat beef very often it's worth the splurge.

Here's my recipe for Boiled Beef: Put the meat in a heavy Dutch oven. Surround it with veal bones, 1 carrot, 1 small onion, and as much garlic as you like—I like lots. I also add a few dried *porcini*, which give the beef the most marvelous flavor and perfume my house as nothing else. Some people tie up little bags of black peppercorns, allspice, and cloves. Others simply stick a few cloves into an onion and put in the peppercorns and allspice, trusting that guests will not eat them.

Cover the beef with bottled springwater or filtered water. I do not recommend tap water unless yours is untreated and pure as glass. Where I live the tap gives out the unmistakable scent of chlorine. In other parts of the country—Philadelphia, for instance—the water tastes of any number of nasty things.

Cover the pot, put it into a gentle oven (300° F.), and leave it there until the beef is tender. This takes from 3 to 5 hours.

When the beef is done, remove it with a big fork and strain the stock through cheesecloth. Clean out the pot and then put everything back in. At this stage you can either serve the beef as is or you can poach some more vegetables in the broth.

I like the beef and the vegetables together in a big soup plate, and I like to serve lots of condiments alongside—mustard; Indian lime pickle, which is quite fiery; horseradish; *cornichons;* pickled onions; and *salsa verde.* This covers the waterfront, internationally speaking, but all these things go well with boiled beef, so why not give your friends a choice?

If you want to be elegant, you can serve the broth as soup and the meat and vegetables as the second course. This makes for more silverware and plates, and I say to hell with it. What you want is a comforting meal on a chilly night, not a lot of work.

After your boiled beef is all eaten up, you need something light, acidic, and astringent. A salad of sliced cucumbers with plenty of dill dressed with a vinaigrette that contains celery salt is very nice. Or an *arugula* salad. Apple crisp or poached pears would make a satisfying end to this meal.

Now what if you want the beef but you do not want veal bones or vegetables or any work whatsoever? You do not want to fuss. One trip to the butcher, one pan, and no work. A long time ago I had a friend who had a husband who had an aunt named Gladys. She lived on a fruit farm and was responsible for huge meals while running the farm as well. Her recipe for Oven-Roasted Beef, known to friends of this family as Aunt Gladys, is a friend to every hardworking person who has a million things to do and people coming for dinner.

Her recipe is stupefyingly simple, foolproof, and also very good: Get a large, very thick chuck steak from the butcher. (The original recipe calls for something called California chuck steak, but a regular old one will do as well.) Take this steak and put it in a large baking dish. Season it with salt and pepper and cover it very tightly with tin foil. Stick it in a 275° F. oven and leave it for 6 hours.

Serve the beef in the evening to a lot of hungry farm workers or to hungry nonfarm workers with a big loaf of bread, some mustard, and some sliced tomatoes (this was, in fact, a summer dish). Sit down, tuck in.

You have one pot to wash, no work to take credit for, and a splendid meal for all.

How to Make Yogurt

There are those who love yogurt and those who loathe it and those who like the flavored kind, which to purists is not yogurt at all.

I am addicted to plain yogurt, and my daughter developed a craving for goat's milk yogurt. This delicious stuff, made by Coach Farms in Pine Plains, New York, comes in little plastic four-ounce pots and costs about a dollar. This did not seem to me much of an expense until I realized that a small child can eat three of these a day. I decided that I would go to the health food store and buy some goat's milk and make my own yogurt, which I had been told was the easiest thing in the world, almost as easy as having a baby.

The world is full of earth-mother types who are happy to tell you that having a baby is a snap and that yogurt is simply a matter of putting cold milk in a warm place with a little leftover yogurt added as a starter. My oldest friend's mother, who, in fact, is no cook at all, made yogurt for years. If she could do it, surely I could do it, I said.

I bought half a gallon of ready-made yogurt and began to read.

The first recipe, definitely in the earth-mother camp, told me to boil some milk and cool it down till I could stick my index finger in it for ten seconds, put in the starter, and place the whole thing in a bowl in a warm place wrapped in a towel.

I did as I was told, and the result, while delicious, was more like soup. Then I began to ask around. My friends who had made yogurt had never gotten it thick, except with a yogurt maker, although they all knew old ladies and gentlemen who made flawless yogurt with nothing more than a glass bowl and an old sweater.

I tried again, this time using Claudia Roden's *Middle Eastern Cookery*. This book straightened me out on a few points, ratio of yogurt to milk being one of them. Mrs. Roden does not use towels to keep her yogurt warm: She uses shawls.

My yogurt, while delicious, was still thin.

I turned to *Joy of Cooking* and was told that I should get some foam rubber and cut it to fit around the bowl I was going to use, and that a thermometer was a good idea. This told me something I needed to know: You have to keep the milk hot to make yogurt.

Then I went to my local flea market looking for the ideal vessel to make yogurt in. What I found was a Mason-type jar made of heavy milk glass. I brought it home, washed it, and tried again.

This time I set the jar over the pilot light for a while wrapped in a striped receiving blanket. Then I got chicken, thinking the whole thing was too hot, so I put it in the oven, which is a warm, but not very warm place.

The result was more like yogurt than like soup, and it was clear that I was on the right track. Yogurt, however, is like fried chicken: It takes lots of practice to get it right. And so while I do not have it quite right, I know that I will be spending many years making yogurt, and I feel that I have combed through the recipes to cull the best of each. Yogurt *is* about as easy as having a baby, but it is cheaper and less painful:

1. First of all, buy the most delicious yogurt you can find. The better the starter, the better the yogurt, although homemade yogurt is always more delicious than even the most delicious store-bought yogurt by virtue of being so fresh.

2. Select the kind of milk you want: Goat's milk makes the best yogurt, in my opinion, and it is slightly more tart than cow's milk. One of the most memorable yogurts I have ever eaten was made with half milk and half cream, but you can also use low-fat milk. Skimmed milk should never be used, as it is too thin and watery to begin with.

3. Heat the milk to a boil, let it froth up, and then simmer for 2 minutes. Take it off the stove and let it cool down. 110° F. is the temperature to cool it to, at which point you can keep your index finger in it for ten seconds. If you have an index finger, you probably do not need a thermometer.

4. The proportion of milk to yogurt is 2½ cups to 1 tablespoon. Beat some of the warm milk into the starter, then add the rest of the milk. Use a whisk to beat all the yogurt into the milk.

5. The best vessel for yogurt is glass, which holds heat better. A jar is preferable to a bowl. A Mason-type jar is ideal. Pour the yogurt into the jar, wrapped with an old sweater or towel or baby blanket or shawl, and put it on top of the pilot light overnight.

The next morning, put it in the fridge and let it cool down. In the afternoon you should have yogurt of some consistency or other.

When I was growing up, yogurt was eaten by food faddists and Europeans. Health food stores were few and far between. They smelled funny and were inhabited by people with long braids or truman shirts, wearing sandals and socks.

The sixties changed all that. While it is now fashionable to knock the counterculture, we should not forget that it was those long-haired weirdos who gave us, among many other valuable things like the antiwar movement, the natural food movement. Now there is a health food store on almost every corner, and we can have whole-grain bread, unsprayed apples, and free-running chickens. We can also buy yogurt at the supermarket.

I first tasted yogurt in Paris when I was eighteen at a student cafeteria. It came with the meal in a little glass pot. It was not considered a sweet. It was something you ate, say, with lentils or lamb stew.

I have tried flavored yogurt and yogurt with fruit in it, but that is not yogurt to me. I like mine plain, or with something savory, such as eggplant. I also love laban, or yogurt cheese, which is easily made at home by dumping a container of yogurt into a strainer lined with cheesecloth or a linen napkin. Place a plate on the top, and a weight on the plate. In a few hours, the whey is pressed out of the curd, and you are left with yogurt cheese. As there is now something called no-fat yogurt, you can serve this cheese to friends on low-fat diets. Some people leave laban alone. Some flavor it with herbs, and some roll it into little balls, spice it up, and put it in olive oil.

And for those who crave sweets, homemade yogurt over blueberries is probably close to heaven. Even the militantly anti-fruit-in-yogurt set sit still for that.

The Case of the Mysterious Flatbread

One sunny spring day I took my daughter to a park in lower Manhattan. In front of the gate sat an elderly woman wearing what looked to be a sari and selling little pastry triangles out of a brightly colored woven basket. A small handwritten sign read, I thought, "Samosas." She was also selling large disklike breads, identified only by an uninformative sticker proclaiming "all natural."

I pointed to the breads. "What are those?" I asked.

"Two dollar fifty cents," she said.

"Did you make them?"

"Two dollar fifty cents," she replied.

I tried one more time. "What do you call them?"

"Two dollar fifty cents," she said with a pleasant smile.

Like the bird-woman in *Mary Poppins*—who can only say "Feed the birds! Tuppence a bag!"—the woman selling flatbreads in the park seemed to know just one phrase in English.

"Maybe it won't be very good," I said to myself hopefully as I tucked one of these breads into my bag, "and then I won't be unhappy that I have no idea what it is and can never replicate it in my own kitchen."

Before I met my husband, I never gave bread much thought. Like many Americans I had felt it was the proper endpaper for a sandwich but hardly a thing in itself. My husband was born in Europe, and for him bread is the staff of life. I now realize that our diet consists of about 40 percent bread. Our daughter is a veritable bread omnivore. We eat *focaccia,* tortillas, *chapati,* bannock, potato bread, semolina loaves, and homemade whole-wheat *baguettes.* When our daughter was about three, she uttered this memorable sentence: "Mommy, go to Balducci's and get me some goat yogurt and a garlic sourdough bread."

It was with a doubting heart that I sliced this Indian bread (or whatever it was) for Sunday night supper.

Unfortunately it was wonderful—spongy and light, speckled with tiny, black onion seeds. It had the aspect of a giant griddle scone and some of the texture of an English muffin. Because I happen to have a nice, round griddle, I decided to take a shot at it.

First I searched through my Indian cookbooks. Most Indian breads are not leavened, but this one appeared to be, and so I figured if I hit a recipe that called for leavening I had struck gold.

In a crumbling little volume entitled *Indian Cooking* by Savitri Chowdhary, published in Britain in 1954, I found a recipe for something called *khamiri moti roti,* which is made with a curd starter for which I substituted yogurt. The starter and flour mixture is supposed to sit in a warm place for eighteen hours, but after eighteen hours it looked much the same as it had eighteen hours before—not a good sign.

The resulting bread did not rise at all after twenty-four hours, but I nonetheless toasted it on my griddle. It *looked* very like what I had brought home from the park but had the texture of underbaked clay or layers of waterlogged parchment.

Undaunted, I did not give up. I tried it again, this time using a teaspoon of yeast, and met with howling success.

Here then, for anyone who wants to make a delicious, exotic, and really easy bread (or an attractive pile of biscuits) is the method for Flatbread.

Stir together 2 tablespoons of warm water with a teaspoon of yeast and 2 tablespoons of yogurt. Mix in ⅓ cup of flour and 2 teaspoons of sugar. Leave overnight, or all morning, or for 3 hours in an unlit oven. The mixture will bubble nicely until you are ready for it.

In a bowl combine 2 cups of flour, 2 teaspoons of sea salt, and 1 tablespoon of black onion seeds (these are called *kalaunji*). Add the yogurt starter and 1 cup of warm water. Knead the dough on a floured board, kneading in an additional ¾ cup flour, and leave it to rise for 2 hours.

When the dough has doubled in bulk, divide it in half. Heat the griddle until it is hot. Flatten the dough as for pizza or roll it out and turn it onto the griddle. You want the bread to toast but not burn. When it is brown and speckled on both sides (this takes about 5 minutes), reduce the heat to low and continue to cook it for about 10 minutes. Tap it to see if it sounds hollow.

This bread is flat and spongy and goes with anything you can think of. And it takes less than a half hour of hands-on work to produce. Furthermore, flatbread proves that we are all brothers and sisters. It is a cross between a Scottish griddle scone, an English muffin, a Russian bialy, an Italian *focaccia,* and a Navajo fry bread—a whole United Nations in one loaf, and cheap and delicious besides.

It is embarrassing to admit the pride I took in tracking this thing down. While I was not patting myself on the back, I was ordering such tomes as *Rotis and Naans of India* by Mrs. Purobi Babbar from Kitchen Arts and Letters, Manhattan's four-star cookbook store.

A few weeks later I went back to the park, and there was the woman with her basket. I decided to try to engage her in conversation, but first I thought I would buy some "Samosas." It was when I looked at the sign closely that I saw that they were not *samosas* at all. They were called "Sambusa." It occurred to me that I might not have been on the right track after all.

I pointed to the bread. "*Roti?*" I said.

She looked at me uncomprehendingly.

"Where are you from? What is your country?" I asked.

She gave me a big smile. She pointed to herself and to the bread. "Ethiopia!" she said.

Well, of course, we *are* all brothers and sisters. This bread from Ethiopia is very similar to a bread from India or Scotland and is appreciatively devoured by a nice Jewish girl from Philadelphia, her husband, who was born in Latvia, and their New Yorker daughter.

Coffee

I come from a coffee-loving family, and you can always tell if my sister and I have been around, because both of us collect all the dead coffee from everyone's morning cup, pour it over ice, and drink it. This is a disgusting habit, and only a coffee addict would indulge in it.

Many years ago, at a Viennese restaurant, I discovered the coffee ice cube. From then on, as soon as the weather got hot, I brewed a pot of coffee, cooled it down, poured it into ice trays, and had the luxury of iced coffee which was *never* diluted. This shows, I feel, how far gone a person can get.

My mother used to use the Silex method of brewing coffee, one that is fascinating to young children, since the coffee goes up a glass bulb and then down (or the reverse—I can no longer keep it straight). She found this easier to cope with than the Chemex, which is practically idiot-proof, although the wooden girdle, which wraps around the glass and gives you a handhold, always falls off. I myself disdain Chemex coffee in favor of the Melitta, which is made of fairly breakproof porcelain, except that the handle always breaks on the gizmo you put the filter papers in, and it is hard to get replacements.

As a blithe youth, when most of my friends were either drinking their heads off or spending their money on recreational drugs, I parceled out a little extra money so I could buy pure Colombian coffee (in a can) and brew it up in the exceptionally nasty little percolator that came with my furnished apartment.

The percolator, as any coffee nut knows, is the worst way to brew coffee, but it smells the best. That gorgeous, comforting, mellow *brown* aroma of perking coffee is caused by the dispersal through the air of all that makes coffee delicious. What you are left with is a muddy beverage, often tasting of boiled sugar sacks, and a delicious-smelling room. In my life I have only known one person who knew what to do with a percolator. This friend, who was brought up in Cuba, dumped Medaglia d'Oro espresso into her electric perk, boiled up milk, and poured hot milk and a kind of burnt coffee sludge together. It was one of the best cups of coffee I have ever had.

My coffee breakthrough happened when someone gave me a little Krups grinder and a bag of beans. Fresh beans seemed to me so significantly more delicious that I was hooked and have been ever since. I began to look for the best freshly roasted beans, and I kept them in a glass jar in the refrigerator. Every two weeks I cleaned my grinder to prevent the intrusion of so much as one rancid coffee speck. When I came near to running out of coffee I did not feel really secure until I had a fresh supply.

I discovered that mocha java, a very nice coffee, was magnificent chilled, which brought the chocolate flavor out. I found myself less inclined toward what is called American roast (or brown roast) and much more drawn to Italian and French roasts, the heat of those processes bringing out the oils and making the beans shiny and fragrant. Then I discovered Vienna roast—somewhere in between brown and French roast—and drank it all day long out of an oversized French cup.

Then I got pregnant. Coffee in quantity is not good for the developing fetus. Of course, coffee in the amounts I used to drink it is also terrible for developed people, and so I cut back. I was allowed one cup of coffee a day, and it seemed to me the height of pleasure and luxury to stretch out in bed with my coffee, and watch the saucer jiggle on my stomach as the developing fetus kicked it around. Having cut back to one cup, I began to realize what a strong drug caffeine really is, and nowadays a cup of coffee in the afternoon disturbs my sleep at night. But I would not give up that morning cup for anything.

It was as a nursing mother that I discovered decaffeinated espresso. My baby was not terribly interested in sleeping, and it seemed a dumb idea to pep her up by jolting her with caffeine, but I knew if I did not have a cup of coffee at my six o'clock wake-up, I would never make it through the day. Decaffeinated coffee was a revelation. It tasted pretty much like coffee, and it smelled like coffee, and it perked me up as coffee will.

I like my coffee with milk and sugar—a child's teaspoon of sugar will do. I do not like cream in coffee. I am also fond of coffee with chicory and hot milk, café con leche, café au lait, and cappuccino, which was one of my child's first words. On the other hand, I have never been mad for anything coffee flavored, although some people are passionately fond of coffee desserts. Recently I came across an easy coffee dessert which is also delicious.

Coffee Fluff

1. Make 1 cup of double-strength coffee. French roast is good for this.
2. If you do not use a filter method, filter the coffee and add 2 tablespoons of sugar and 1 tablespoon gelatin. Stir until the gelatin dissolves. Chill until thick and soupy and beginning to set.
3. Whip ½ pint of cream. Whip the coffee jelly until frothy and stir the coffee and the cream together.
4. Pour into a wet mold or wet custard cups.
5. Serve with a little shaved chocolate on the top.

All coffee lovers must have in their possession a book entitled *Coffee*, by Claudia Roden, published by Penguin, from which the above recipe was adapted. It makes fascinating and agreeable bedtime reading for addicts unable to sleep, or those sitting around at two o'clock in the morning sipping an iced coffee and wondering why they are so wakeful.

Not a day goes by that we are not given a list of things that are bad for us. These lists, which always mention coffee right away, are usually published in the health column of the daily paper, which we read as we drink our morning coffee.

I have gone without coffee. I did not get the jitters or begin to drool. Nor did I lose my memory or regain lost energy. I simply missed that wonderful taste, that sweet, pungent smell, that warm feeling in my chest. After a few days I cried out, like the maiden in Bach's Coffee Cantata (it has always made perfect sense to me that a great composer would devote a piece of music to this subject):

> Coffee! Coffee! *I must have it.*
> *If I do not have coffee I will die!*

About Biscuits

I have come to believe that anyone who walks into a kitchen should know how to make biscuits. Biscuits are the utility infielder of the culinary world: They serve as bread, as snacks, as something to nibble with cocktails. You can use them for shortcake or pizza crusts, or pile them up with peaches and make a sweet pizza. They can be plain, spicy, savory, or sweet. You can eat them hot or cold, and furthermore, they closely resemble their first cousin (or twin sister), the scone. You can use them for sandwiches or serve them with soup. There is nothing in this world as useful or as delicious.

Of course you can always add water or milk to a mix. I have done this, and the resulting biscuits tasted so very much like salty laundry powder that I never tried again. Or you can buy one of those paper tubes that you smack against the counter and then find yourself gnashing your teeth trying to pull apart. The contents resemble marshmallows. When you bake them they are sweet and puffy. With no heft or spirit, they are flabby and tasteless.

Real biscuits are a *snap*. A child can make them. Once you get the hang of them, which takes about two seconds, they take about seven seconds, so to speak.

These flaky, delicate, and melting little buns are composed of almost nothing at all. Everything they are made of is commonly found around the house (unless you are one of those people whose fridge contains a bottle of Champagne and a lime).

You need 2 cups of flour, ½ stick of butter or margarine (or a combination of the two), 2 teaspoons of baking powder, and ¾ cup (a little more or less depending on the flour and the weather) of milk—sweet, sour, or buttermilk (or a combination of milk and yogurt).

Rub the butter into the flour and baking powder. I myself have had unhappy experiences with pastry blenders and feel that your hands do the best job, but if you don't feel like doing this by hand, two knives work fine. When the butter is well blended add the milk until you have a not-too-sticky dough. Turn it out on a floured board and knead about five times. Roll, cut out, and bake at 400° F. for about 15 minutes until golden. Some people like their biscuits just baked, which means that they will be a floury white. Some people like their biscuits crispy and a little browner than golden. However you like them, they will never fail you.

I am a fool for a biscuit cutter and have a tiny collection of them. You can find them in cookware stores, or if you are a flea marketer like me, you can pick them up for under a dollar. But because biscuits are so user-friendly and agreeable, you can cut them out with a drinking glass, or roll out a square or round and cut them with a knife. You do not need to butter the cookie sheet you bake them on. They go on the sheet as is, but if you are a stickler, kitchen parchment paper (one of the truly great conveniences of life) keeps you from getting even the merest crumb to clean up.

In the back of Edna Lewis's immortal classic *The Taste of Country Cooking* is a word of advice about baking powder. Mrs. Lewis feels that double-acting baking powder, the kind now generally available, leaves a bitter aftertaste, and she is right. She suggests making your own with 2 parts cream of tartar to 1 part baking soda. Since I read this piece of advice I have never looked back. What is good for Mrs. Lewis is good for the nation, in my opinion.

Furthermore, I feel that baking powder, like yeast, is a potent force, and should be used sparingly. I have made biscuits according to recipes calling for as much as 1 tablespoon. They were light and fluffy and had a definite sour under taste. I have made biscuits with as little as 1 teaspoon, and they were light, too. I have made them with sweet milk, half-and-half, and buttermilk, but the best I ever made were made with milk that had gone naturally sour. Instead of throwing it out, I used it to make the biscuit dough for a tomato pie, and it was celestial.

There is no end to the things you can put in biscuit dough. Chives are nice, and so are toasted sesame seeds, or poppy seeds. You can add Parmesan or grated Cheddar cheese and spike them with cayenne pepper. You can toast up cumin seeds and add those, too, or snip some fresh rosemary. You can add a tablespoon of sugar and a handful of raisins, and turn them into scones.

For a picnic you can take the dough, roll it out, place it carefully on a baking sheet or baking stone, brush it with olive oil and tomato sauce, layer it with thin-sliced tomatoes, and scatter any kind of cheese on top. This sort of biscuit pizza is excellent topped with fried peppers, crisp-fried eggplant, or zucchini. You can brush it with pesto and put on top of it almost anything you can think of. It takes a few minutes to throw it together, and it looks very impressive when you take it out of the oven.

This summer I discovered another use for the ever-helpful biscuit and used it all summer long: as dessert. To the basic dough you add 1 generous tablespoon of sugar. Roll out and spread with the jelly or jam of your choice. On top of the jelly arrange in some attractive pattern juicy, sliced fruit. I have used peaches, plums, and nectarines.

I have not tried apples or pears with this, since they seem too subtle. You want something acidic and very sweet. Scatter the top with sugar (I used Demerara, a large-crystal sugar available in specialty foods stores), and you might chop up some walnuts and add them, too. Bake for about 20 minutes and serve hot, cold, or lukewarm.

This is the sort of dish I love best: easy, plain, but very delicious, and absolutely gorgeous to look at. Your friends will think that you have been slaving over a hot stove all day long. If you don't love them dearly, let them think so. If they are your close, personal friends and have a few minutes to spare, take them in the kitchen with you and show them what a breeze the whole operation is.

And if your friends don't cook, so be it. You have the satisfaction of giving them something down-home and really delicious, something that expresses your fondness for them. And when the biscuits have all been eaten, or the tomato pizza has vanished, and the last crumb of the plum tart has been consumed, and you modestly remark that it was no effort at all, they look at you hungrily, and with flinty eyes, and say: "If it's so easy, please go make some more, right now."

Down-Home Standbys

There are times in life—usually after a spate of self-indulgence—when one's soul cries out for minimalist food: clean, plain, and nontaxing. A piece of grilled fish, some blanched asparagus, and perhaps the merest morsel of goat cheese with a very underdressed salad are just what the doctor ordered. But there are other times, usually in horrible weather, when one longs for straightforward, savory, down-home food, and lots of it. This is the sort of cooking people call "heartwarming," and there is no doubt about it—it *does* cheer people up.

I have four standby dishes in this category. I love them so much that I even cook them in the summer and eat them cold. They are Inez Fontenez's Succotash; Lima Beans with *Chorizo* (spicy pork sausage); Polenta with Hot Pepper; and Broccoli Soup with Curry.

Inez Fontenez is from the southern part of Florida. A hard-working woman and a deacon in her church, she claims not to like to cook, but the first time I tasted her pickled peaches I almost began to cry with happiness. When she brought me a jar of her succotash to try, I felt that I had floated away. This is an odd reaction to succotash, but there you are.

Succotash is normally a humble food: lima beans and corn, dressed up by New England cooks with a splash of cream and a scrape of nutmeg—a nice, simple side dish. Mrs. Fontenez's succotash is nothing like this. It is what succotash can be if it really tries hard. I have eaten this hot with roast chicken, all by itself with some jasmine rice, cold from the fridge on a piece of bread, and straight out of the pot without sharing.

Inez Fontenez's Succotash

1. Mrs. Fontenez begins by making what is almost like a Spanish *sofrito:* In a saucepan in a little olive oil she sweats 1 small minced onion, 1 minced garlic clove, 1 minced small red bell pepper (or green if red are not in season), and salt and pepper to taste, covered, over low heat until the onion becomes soft.
2. Then she adds ¼ teaspoon ground ginger, a 10-ounce package frozen corn, a 10-ounce package frozen lima beans, ¼ pound okra, trimmed and cut up, and 1¼ cups water. She simmers the mixture, covered, for 8 minutes, or until the beans are tender, removes the lid, and then simmers the succotash for a few more minutes, or until most of the liquid is evaporated. Serves 4 to 6.

Strange as the ground ginger sounds, it is the snap that pulls this wonderful vegetable stew together. Take it from me, Mrs. Fontenez's succotash is a heavenly thing and a big hit at any gathering—if you haven't eaten it all up yourself with a piece of toast for breakfast.

• • •

I am addicted to lima beans, which I feel have an undeservedly bad reputation. They are pillowy, velvety, and delicious, and people should stop saying mean things about them. I have fed my lima bean and *chorizo* casserole to lima-bean haters with amazing results; there is nothing like a few spicy sausages to put this underrated bean into proper perspective.

Lima Bean and *Chorizo* Casserole

1. Soak ½ pound dried lima beans in cold water to cover overnight, drain and rinse them, put them in a kettle, and cover them with about 4 cups water. Embed in the beans 2 to 3 large garlic cloves (these do not have to be peeled, and garlic lovers might want to add more) and 1 bouillon cube. A bouillon cube is usually a nasty thing, but for some reason it is just right for these beans.

2. Simmer the beans very gently, uncovered, until they are tender; this can take from 45 minutes to 1 hour.

3. When the beans are tender, tip the whole mixture into a casserole, add 4 spicy *chorizes* for 4 people (*kielbasa, andouille,* or the like would be fine, too), and cook the casserole, covered, for 1 hour in a 350° F. oven.

4. Skim off the fat, cut up 1 medium potato into ¼-inch pieces, and lay the pieces on top. Cook the casserole, uncovered, for 45 minutes.

If the idea of beans and potatoes strikes you as odd, I can only say that I fed this to a couple of freezing pals one snowy day and was answered with shouts of joy. Hands down, this is one of the best things I have ever cooked, and, although you would not want it as a steady diet, on a winter night it makes a person feel warm, happy, and well taken care of.

When I am feeling down, I crave polenta. I like the kind that, when cooked, looks like fluffy scrambled eggs and is ever so good topped with Gorgonzola and toasted walnuts. But I also like the kind that you cook, turn into a baking dish, and let congeal. If you are feeding people in suits and ties and dresses, you can cut this with a biscuit cutter and arrange the pieces overlapping in some attractive way, but, if your guests are in blue jeans, you can simply cut it into squares. In either case, put the pieces in a buttered baking dish, dot with butter, scatter with Parmesan, and bake.

Polenta with Hot Pepper

1. Bring 4 cups water to a boil, whisk in 1 cup coarse cornmeal slowly, and stir the mixture constantly with a wooden spoon over moderately low heat for about 30 minutes.
2. Stir in some minced garlic, salt, dried hot red pepper flakes, minced scallion, and a good handful of grated Parmesan. Serves 4.

This polenta is so delicious that I have seen people eat the left-overs cold. And it would be very good with either Mrs. Fontenez's succotash or the lima bean and *chorizo* casserole.

When I am tired or starving (which accounts for most of the time), I make my favorite soup. I have downed gallons of this stuff in every season of the year. It is good hot or cold and making it is as easy as sneezing.

Curried Broccoli Soup

1. Take 1 head of broccoli and 1 medium potato, chop them up, and put them in a kettle. Add 2 garlic cloves and about 5 cups chicken broth. (Vegetarians can use vegetable broth or bouillon. Fresh chicken stock makes a more delicate soup, but canned—especially the low-salt variety, which has better flavor—is all right, too.) Simmer the mixture for about 20 minutes, or until the vegetables are very tender.

2. Add about 1 teaspoon curry powder and simmer the mixture for another 5 minutes. A particularly delicious curry, Turban Brand Curry Powder, can be found in West Indian shops and is worth tracking down. I also once discovered, in a rented house, a bottle of something that looked plain old weird to me: curry powder with dried orange zest. To my amazement, it was just the thing for broccoli soup and can be approximated by

adding the tiniest bit of grated fresh orange zest (about ¼ teaspoon) along with the curry.

3. Transfer the vegetables with a little of the stock to a blender. I like to add about ½ to 1 cup plain nonfat yogurt and then whizz the mixture into a purée. This makes about 6½ cups of soup, enough for 4 people.

Once you have fed this celestial stuff to your loved ones (you might want to leave out the curry when serving children), you will find yourself with a staple on your hands, one that can be quickly made, spiked with hot pepper for grown-ups, and can even be very nice when drunk cold, straight from the fridge.

If you happen to be feeding eccentric people, you might put all four of these dishes on the same menu. I have done it. The meal took place in the country during an ice storm, when the most interesting, tiny hexagonal-shaped pieces of ice fell steadily on the windowpanes, making a kind of hissing noise.

It was definitely *not* an elegant meal. (Mud-splashed Wellies are hardly the proper attire for formal dining.) But it was a very satisfying, lip-smacking meal, after which everyone felt perfectly content. In these trying times, that's about as good as it gets.

More About Gingerbread

When my daughter was two years old I began baking gingerbread on an almost weekly basis. Little children seemed to love it—the spicier the better. For special occasions I would ice this gingerbread with chocolate or lemon frosting. Some days I split it into layers and slathered raspberry jam all over it. The recipe I used was a nice, traditional one from *Charleston Receipts*, the classic cookbook put out by the Junior League of Charleston and full of good things.

A few years later I decided to branch out, and after a while I realized that I was on a quest for the perfect gingerbread. Like most heroic quests, this search has not turned up any ultimates, but the adventure has definitely been worthwhile.

It is amazing how many people are hooked on gingerbread. People who like it love it and crave it. These people are extremely easy to make happy, and they are more than glad to taste the results of your experiments. I generally try out recipes on my daughter (a confirmed gingerbread fiend). My other victim is our friend Dr. David Hunt, a neurosurgeon who lives in Hoboken, New Jersey. His idea of heaven is some good science fiction and a piece of gingerbread.

The sad fact is that gingerbread is on the decline, although it is alive and well in the children's books of the fifties, where cheerful housewives wait at home for the arrival of their hungry children at three o'clock, ready with a great big pan of warm gingerbread and some ice-cold milk.

You do not have to be a housebound mother to make gingerbread. All you need is to put aside an hour or so to mix up the batter and bake it, and then, provided you do not have a huge mob waiting to devour the gingerbread immediately, it will pay you back for a few days because it gets better as it ages. I myself never have any around long enough to age, but my English cookbooks assure me that a few days make all the difference.

After years of hands-on experience, I have come to three conclusions about gingerbread. First, the ground ginger must be fresh. If your half-consumed jar of ginger has dust all over it, throw it out and buy a new one—ginger loses its power after it has been sitting around for nine months or so. If you live near an ethnic market that sells spices in bulk, buy your ground ginger there. Otherwise, a fresh jar from the supermarket will do fine.

Second, most recipes are very timid about the quantity of ginger. You may start out mild and end up doubling or tripling the amount. I like a heaping tablespoon, which may be much too much for some people but not enough for others. This is a matter of taste.

Third, never use ordinary molasses. It is simply too bitter—*not* what you want. Pure cane syrup is the name of the game, and I wholeheartedly endorse that made by the C. S. Steen Syrup Mill of Abbeville, Louisiana, a company that will take mail orders. British recipes often call for black treacle, for which Steen's cane syrup is a good substitute, or light treacle, for which I use Lyle's

Golden Syrup, an English standby that can now be found in many supermarkets and fancy foods shops.

If you happen to be a fan of English cookbooks (I seem to be addicted to them), you will be amazed at the array of gingerbreads, from those dry, breadlike ones called parkin to the dark, sticky ones that are more like what we Americans know as pudding. After much trial and error, I have come across two recipes that are sublime. Nevertheless, I realize hundreds more are out there, yet untried.

The first comes from a British Penguin book, *The Farmhouse Kitchen* by Mary Norwak, which I purchased in a secondhand book shop in Litchfield, Connecticut. It is easy and sensational.

Old-Fashioned Gingerbread

1. Preheat the oven to 375° F. and line the bottom of a buttered 8-inch round tin (2 inches deep) with parchment paper. (Parchment paper has come to have great importance in my kitchen, and it is my opinion that the person who invented it should get a Nobel Prize.)
2. Melt ½ cup cane syrup or black treacle with 6 tablespoons butter.
3. Beat 1 egg with 4 tablespoons buttermilk.
4. Sift together 2 cups flour, 1 teaspoon baking soda, 2 heaping teaspoons ground ginger, 1 teaspoon cinnamon, ⅓ cup firmly packed brown sugar, and a pinch of salt. Mix in ¾ cup dried currants or raisins.
5. Add the egg mixture, then add the syrup mixture, and mix well.

6. Bake 10 minutes in the 375° oven, turn the heat down
   to 325°, and bake 35 to 40 minutes more. A few crumbs
   stick to a tester when the cake is done.

The above recipe is an all-around hit and combines many of
gingerbread's virtues. It is spicy, heartwarming, and cake-like. You
do not need to add one thing: no ice cream, no icing, no poached
fruit on the side. It is really and truly good by itself. For some time
it displaced all others in my kitchen, but people on quests are not
easily satisfied.

After a while I began to long for something new, and in another English book, Delia Smith's *Book of Cakes,* I found what I
was looking for. It is not sticky, but moist and velvety. The name
describes it perfectly:

Damp Gingerbread

1. Preheat the oven to 350° F. Butter a 9-inch round tin
   (2 inches deep) and line the bottom with parchment
   paper.
2. Melt 9 tablespoons butter with 12 ounces (1½ cups)
   Lyle's Golden Syrup.
3. Into a bowl sift 2 cups plus 2 tablespoons flour, ½ teaspoon salt, 1¾ teaspoons baking soda, 1 tablespoon
   ground ginger, ½ teaspoon ground cloves, and ¼ teaspoon cinnamon.
4. Pour the syrup and butter onto the dry ingredients and
   mix well.
5. Add 1 beaten egg and 1 cup milk. Beat well. The batter,

Ms. Smith tells us, will be very liquid, and it is. Pour it into the tin and bake at 350° F. for about 50 to 55 minutes. (The middle should be just set, with the edge pulling away from the pan, and a tester will bring out a few crumbs.) Cool the cake in the tin for 10 minutes before turning out.

This gingerbread went over well with the brain surgeon from Hoboken, who pointed out that in order to do a thorough scientific test he would need to have samples from a great many gingerbreads put before him so that he could, as they say in academic circles, compare and contrast. However, when threatened with being replaced as my tester, he broke down and admitted that it was very, very good.

A Harried Cook's Guide
to Some Fast Food

Some time ago, when I was a young bride, I had endless time to cook and endless time to shop. Anyone delivering a package to my house on the afternoon of a dinner party back then might have found me in the kitchen dicing or slicing or tying up a chicken and rubbing it with a kind of pomade made of butter, garlic, and crushed herbs.

The morning of a dinner party I would curl up in an armchair and think about dessert. I made things like *crème brûlée* with a crackly sugar top, lemon mousse, and Bavarian cream. I turned out lemon curd for a lemon tart. I whipped egg whites in a copper bowl and made Elizabeth David's flourless chocolate cake.

Those days are long gone. There is nothing that puts a crimp in your cooking style like the arrival of a baby. It is hard to whip the egg whites wholeheartedly when at any moment your infant may wake up from her nap and require you. It's also not easy to stuff the chicken breast with something complicated when your darling is crawling on the floor at your feet. And it is impossible to concentrate on a recipe when your seven-year-old calls out a thousand times from the dining room, "Mom, what does this spell?"

Once you have a child, speed and convenience is the name of the game. It is my opinion that you can make a decent dinner speedily and conveniently if you go in for what I call *la cuisine de la "slobbe" raffinée,* or "the cooking of the refined slob."

Take, for example, Roast Chicken, which is almost everyone's favorite dish. I have never seen a menu outside of a vegetarian restaurant that does not list some variety or other of it. In the old days I used to slip herbs and savory things like *porcini* mushrooms under the skin and baste the chicken constantly, but I have gradually come to know that none of these things is necessary.

The refined slob does not, for instance, even tie up her chicken. Her fancy imported linen kitchen string—which she bought at a snooty cooking shop at great expense and which was, she told her family, for trussing the chicken *only*—has been purloined by her child, who has used it to make spiderwebs by tying all the chairs together. Before I had a child, I would no more have cooked an untrussed chicken than I would have reused the dead coffee grounds, but today I know an untrussed chicken is perfectly fine.

As for stuffing, half a lemon or some cloves of garlic work out swell. Wait till your child is in junior high school to make some wonderful mixture of chestnuts and diced prunes. I always dust my roast chicken with paprika. This is a family tradition. Paprika gives a chicken color and taste, and it takes under eight seconds to apply it.

Butter flavored with microscopically minced garlic is great if you have the time, but, if not, take an entire head of garlic, break it into cloves, and throw the cloves into the roasting pan. When the chicken is done, the garlic is too, and the cloves can be slipped out of their skins (the refined slob does not peel the garlic) and spread on bread or merely gobbled down.

If you are particularly harried, it is perfectly acceptable to cut up potatoes you have not bothered to peel along with some carrots and put them in the roasting pan, too. Then you have not only roast chicken but also roasted vegetables. Roasted Vegetables are about the easiest thing in the world to cook and are lovely to eat hot, cold, or lukewarm. People who want to avoid chicken fat can cook them in a companion roasting pan, preferably earthenware or ceramic. Slice the onions, cut up the potatoes quite thin, and slice some red peppers any old way. Put the vegetables in the pan and sprinkle them with salt and pepper (or merely salt, if you are serving this to a child). Drizzle the vegetables with olive oil and roast them next to the chicken for an hour.

I like to roast my chicken at 325° F. for about two hours. I do actually baste when I think about it, but I have also basted only at the last minute and all was well. Then it's just a matter of straining the juices, skimming off the fat, carving up the bird, and there you are.

Scalloped Potatoes go wonderfully with roast chicken. In the old days I took great pains with these, and they never came out the way I liked them. I have since learned a trick from a now-unrecalled magazine article, and I make them in a trice. If you have a food processor you can make them in less than that. The potatoes—say about 2½ pounds—should be cut ⅛ inch thick and then plunged into cold water. Bring 2½ cups of milk to a boil in a large saucepan, pat the potatoes dry, and boil them in the milk until they are barely tender. Add salt to taste and then tip the whole affair—the sludgy milk and the half-cooked potatoes—into a buttered dish. Add garlic if you like it—if not, not—scatter bread crumbs on top, and bake the potatoes in a 400° F. oven for about 15 minutes, or until they are bubbly and brown. (You will have to soak the saucepan for quite a long while—that's boiling milk for you—but it's worth it.)

When I was a little girl, making salad dressing was my chore, and it was an awesome one. Everything had to be measured out scrupulously, including the sugar (which my mother felt was essential). These days my method is to smash a clove of garlic, pour some olive oil on it, and add salt, pepper, and lemon juice. My daughter has now assumed this chore and performs it very well. For people who want kitchen help, I highly recommend children on the cusp of seven for such jobs.

If you eat a lot of salad you might want to save yourself time by expending about four minutes some afternoon and making yourself a jar of Garlic Vinegar, a substance I could not live without. Take a big head of garlic, separate the cloves, and quarter or smash them. You can leave the skins on, which, if the garlic is purple, makes for a nice color. Put the garlic in a jar that you will never use for any other purpose, cover it with the vinegar of your choice, and let the mixture stand for a few days. As you strain off the vinegar, replenish it. Garlic vinegar is wonderful in a green salad and good on beets, in corn salad, on fried fish, or in a salad made from diced leftover flank steak and lentils.

There are few citizens of this land who do not like a brownie. Even people on diets will nibble a small one if it is offered. Brownies are in many ways the ideal dessert. You can eat as many or as few as you wish. And brownies go well with so many things—ice cream, strawberries, poached pears, or whipped cream, for instance.

There are as many brownie recipes as there are flowers in the meadow. Some are fancy, some are plain. Some have nuts, which I consider a bad idea, because children seem to hate them and end up picking them out and getting brownie crumbs all over everything. I also have several friends with fatal nut allergies, and so I leave nuts out. I have been served brownies with chocolate chips and brownies with raisins, but what most people want is plain old brownies. Some people like their brownies on the cakey side, and some feel they should be more like fudge. I myself like brownies that are what I call "slumped" and the English call "squidgy," which means slightly undercooked but not quite runny in the center.

The best recipe I have for brownies comes from a friend who got it from a magazine article about Katharine Hepburn. It is, apparently, her family's recipe. If there were no other reason to admire Katharine Hepburn, this pan of brownies would be enough to make you worship her.

Katharine Hepburn's Brownies

1. Melt together 1 stick butter and 2 squares unsweetened chocolate and take the saucepan off the heat.
2. Stir in 1 cup sugar, add 2 eggs and ½ teaspoon vanilla, and beat the mixture well.
3. Stir in ¼ cup all-purpose flour and ½ teaspoon salt. (In the original recipe, 1 cup chopped walnuts is added here as well.)

4. Bake the brownies in a buttered and floured 8-inch-square pan at 325° F. for about 40 minutes.

You can cut these brownies into squares, once they have cooled, and eat them out of the pan, but it is so much nicer to pile them on a fancy plate, from which people are going to eat them with their hands anyway. If you want to smarten up your act you can put a square of brownie on a plate with a little blob of *crème fraîche* and a scattering of shaved chocolate.

A dinner of roast chicken, roasted vegetables, scalloped potatoes, salad, and brownies is a festive meal. In certain lights it might even be seen as *elegant*. And as you sit with your feet up, listening to the hum of the dishwasher (or perhaps of some person other than yourself washing the dishes), you can pat yourself on the back for having produced such a feast with a minimum of work. Everyone will think you are wonderful for having made this monumental effort on their behalf. And when they tell you this, you can lean back with a wan smile and say, with some truth: "It was nothing."

The Beet Goes On

It is amazing how many adults loathe beets—although puréed, strained beets are a staple of the baby-food industry. Perhaps in later life the inner child in the grown-up jumps to its feet and says: "You expect me to eat something *magenta?*" Colorwise, the closest you can get is a pomegranate—hardly a common item, and connected in my mind with spitting little seeds into a sink. Beets, however, are abundant, cheap, easy to abuse, and, therefore, easy to hate. Many cooks avoid them because they turn everything pink, including fingernails. The very qualities we may love in a Russian Easter egg are less than attractive on your best white T-shirt.

One of the simplest things to do with a beet is to scrub it gently with a vegetable brush, roll it in a little olive oil, salt, and pepper, and bake it in the oven like a potato. This results in a slightly smoky taste and—in addition to being easy—does not turn your fingers red. When cooked, diced, mixed with bitter endive, and dressed with a creamy vinaigrette, the beet also makes a great salad.

Among the prettiest dinners I ever ate was one that included beets, making me realize that a magenta-colored vegetable can be a real plus when it comes to the art of food arrangement. One hot summer evening, my husband and I hopped on the Hampton Jitney and emerged, starving, at some Hampton or other, where we were picked up by a painter friend of ours, who took us home and fed us a painterly meal: a lobster salad, creamy pink; a plate of light green greens; and a heavy white platter containing steamed broccoli and sliced boiled beets—the one a deep pure green, the other a deep clear fuchsia. The vegetables were served with a garlic and cranberry mayonnaise. It takes a painter to show off something as striking and vibrant as a beet.

Even people who hate beets will sometimes eat borscht, which, when cold, brings the right suave, chilly note to a sultry evening and, when hot, warms the spirit on a frosty winter night. I love it both ways.

Cold borscht can be made with cooked, cut-up beets, chicken stock, and a squirt of lime juice. The mixture is put into the blender with yogurt or buttermilk. It can be spiked with cumin and served with dill, scallions, or nothing at all. For a party, a blob of *crème fraîche* and a pinch of minced chives on each serving is a nice touch.

Hot borscht can be made with meat or not. My particular favorite is one with which I attempt to reproduce the wonderful borscht I have had in the Ukrainian coffee shops on Manhattan's Lower East Side—a thick soup of beets, green beans, white beans, onions, carrots, and beef in a rich beef broth. There is nothing in the world quite like it. This is a one-dish meal when served with bread, a little cheese, a salad, and a glass of beer. It also cooks itself on a back burner and thus is a friend to busy people.

Fancy restaurants have taken to serving something called beet risotto: Arborio rice cooked with stock, beet juice, and beets sautéed in olive oil. I have never tasted it, but the idea of beets with rice made me wonder if beets wouldn't also be wonderful with pasta.

Last summer, with organic beets in profusion, I set to work and have since become addicted to Beets with Angel's Hair Pasta, described by my husband as "weird but successful." I have fed it to children, teenagers, and people with very conservative taste buds with great success. Furthermore, it is ridiculously simple, but you must use juicy early-summer beets.

Take about 4 medium-sized beets and about 8 ounces of dried pasta for 3 or 4 people. Slice and dice the raw beets up fine. (Since it is ease of preparation we are after, it is not necessary to peel the beets. Just cut away any nasty bits, scrub the beets with a soft brush, and dice them.) Mince 1 big clove of garlic into microscopic bits. Throw the beets into a pan with about 2 tablespoons olive oil. Sprinkle the beets with salt and pepper to taste and cook them over moderate heat, stirring. When the beets are just tender add the garlic and cook the mixture for about 1 minute. Add ½ cup chicken broth and simmer the mixture until the beets are tender. Stir in some minced red onion, a little chopped rosemary, and some crushed dried hot red pepper flakes. Then spoon the mixture over the angel's hair pasta with lots of freshly grated Parmesan.

The whole business takes about half an hour, which means that a person can come home from work and have dinner on the table, even dinner for friends, in under an hour. I have also made the dish with a pinch of curry or with a chopped-up tomato. This sauce is *versatile*. I could probably eat pasta with beets every night of my life, with steamed beet greens on the side, tossed with a garlic and ginger dressing. Last summer I lived on the pasta and went around with lurid-colored fingers all season.

If you do not want to ruin your manicure, you might instead make Scarlet Eggs from Sylvia Thompson's wonderful book, *Feasts and Friends: Recipes from a Lifetime.* Hard-boil 7 of the smallest eggs you can find and peel them. Cook 12 of the tenderest little beets you can find in water to cover, peel them, and reserve 1 cup of the cooking liquid. Stick a large bunch of fresh tarragon in the bottom of a jar, fill the jar with the eggs and the beets, and cover them with the reserved cooking liquid and 3 to 4 tablespoons sugar dissolved in 2 cups red-wine vinegar. Add salt and pepper and a couple of cloves of garlic, sliced. Keep the mixture in the refrigerator for a week.

When you slice these fragrant eggs you will find that the whites have turned an amazing shade of red and that the yolks have become a brilliant yellow. In addition to being delicious, these eggs are *beautiful.* Arrange the eggs and the beets on a bed of spinach and call the photographers at once.

Catering on One Dollar a Head

One of the greatest shocks you will ever have is to realize how much it costs to get married on the cheap.

When I got married, two kind friends offered us their loft to get married in. Our judge was an old friend of my husband's. Therefore we did not have to pay for space or legalization. We got married at three in the afternoon and, having fainted dead away at the price per person at nice restaurants, decided to have a small afternoon buffet, Champagne, and wedding cake. For the effort it took you would have thought we were getting married in Central Park and then feeding thousands of people a seven-course meal.

It is mean to think of your family and friends as "heads," but that is how you end up thinking after the caterer has told you how much the tea sandwiches, the almond *tuiles,* the Champagne, and the salmon mousse are going to cost per head. Suddenly you are forced to contemplate what heads must roll to meet the budget—an unlovely thought.

Then you go to the cheerful bakery where you have had such nice petits fours and madeleines and discover that wedding cake is charged per person. Suddenly you contemplate your friends, each with a plate in hand, guzzling *your* wedding cake at great personal expense to you. And then the caterer reminds you that glasses, garbage bags, servers, and cleaners have not yet been included, and suddenly what you thought was going to be a minimalist experience is going to be a major production.

This summer my friend Don Bracken, a painter of West Cornwall, Connecticut, decided to have a studio opening for his new work, and his wife, Janice, decided that you can't ask people to come and look at paintings if you don't give them something to eat or drink. Like everyone else in the world she did not want to spend a ton of money, and so I offered to help. Catering well on the cheap is a subject dear to my heart as well as an intellectual challenge. Janice allowed as how she wanted to make some boat-shaped hors d'oeuvres she had seen in a magazine. I took a dim view of this.

In the first place, she had never made them before, and a cardinal rule of self-catering is, Never try out something you have never made before on a large (or small, for that matter) number of people. Furthermore, she is a public health nurse, a member of the ambulance and fire squad, and the mother of two. I did not see how she, even with help, could make that many boat-shaped hors d'oeuvres for that many people in the two seconds of spare time she (like most mothers) has. I said it was a poor idea.

She said she was tired of large pieces of cheese on wooden boards: Besides, we had done that the year before for another studio opening, and one of her dogs had jumped on the table and eaten a large hole in the cheese and put muddy paw-prints on the beautiful white tablecloth. I had fixed this up by taking the cheese and turning it over so you couldn't see the side the dog had eaten. She felt *this* was a poor idea: unsanitary due to what my daughter calls "dog lick," but she had no choice. Cheese, she felt, was too boring.

Salsa was mentioned. She makes an awesome *salsa*, but another cardinal rule of self-catering is, Never serve anything that *drips*. This is a very good rule if you have good rugs, but even if you don't it is unattractive to watch your guests forced to lick parts of your hors d'oeuvres off their arms.

A large number of small things was then proposed, batted around, and shot down. First of all, a large number of small things adds up. A small number of large things makes much better economic sense.

Another important rule of self-catering is, Unless you have billions of dollars, tons of time, and some real food geniuses happy to help you for nothing, serve a few delicious things in large quantity. Naturally, when giving a party one dreams of plain black trays carried by plainly dressed young men and women containing quail eggs, pea pods that have been split open and filled with some delicious cream cheese, and tiny little shrimp quiches. When you finish with this sort of thing there is nothing left for college tuition or a new roof.

The challenge here was to find something interesting, cheap, and wonderful. Something novel that everyone would like. In this last regard we failed. We provided something not interesting or novel but delicious and cheap, but everyone liked it. Our menu for fifty people was *hummus, pita* bread, *tabbouleh* salad, and the cheese mix from the recipe of my long ago and sainted Viennese baby-sitter, and, because so much sour cream had been bought, we made a blue cheese and sour cream dip.

The Viennese cheese mix is made by mixing cream cheese and sour cream (a low-fat version of both is available)—2 packages of cream cheese and 1 large container sour cream. To this you add 1 tablespoon of paprika and 1 of celery salt plus about 2 table-spoons of capers.

There was almost nothing left at the end of this do except one small bowl of *tabbouleh* salad. The *hummus* was made the day before, as were the cheese mix and the dip. The *tabbouleh* salad was made at the last minute, except that the parsley and scallions and dressing were chopped and made the night before. The remaining Bracken dog (the cheese eater had found another home) was not interested in any of these items, and so things could be arranged way beforehand.

In addition to being cheap, this spread was *easy* and not time-intensive. And so to the list of cardinal rules I add the following:

1. Unless you are that sort of person, don't drive yourself nuts.
2. Realize that people are made happy by delicious food, and you do not have to knock yourself out to be thrilling or original.
3. If you are going to make a large quantity of *hummus*, use your food processor or borrow that of a friend.
4. Always buy more lemons than you think you need.
5. Think small.
6. Even if you associate putting together a party with chaos and panic, remember this startling idea: You can actually have fun at your own party.

Real Food for Tots

There is nothing trickier than writing about food for kids. People have nothing but notions about this. Naturally they think theirs are better than yours, and I feel that mine are better than theirs. This subject is loaded with crotchets, biases, and hidden agendas.

Therefore I feel I must come straight out of the closet and announce that I am what not so nice persons might call a food crank. I believe in all those good things food cranks believe in; breast-feeding, homemade baby food, the baby-food grinder. When my daughter became a toddler and began to consume large quantities of apple juice, I mail-ordered her juice from Walnut Acres, an organic farm. I did not want to lie in bed all night worrying about alar. The fact is that our children are ingesting pesticides and additives that did not exist when we were children, and we have no idea what their long-range effect will be.

As a bona fide food crank I made the assumption that unless I make it, or buy it from a local source, or am convinced of its purity, it probably isn't pure. This is an extreme stance, and naturally I am not consistent. I buy tomato paste from Italy that comes in a tube, as well as all kinds of Italian pasta. I don't know what is in them, but I buy them anyway. I don't know where the milk in the Parmesan cheese comes from. My theory is, Provision as much pure and organic food as you can and let the rest go by.

I am, of course, a moving target. I work at home, and therefore if I go to the greenmarket in the morning to buy organic eggs and milk, no one is going to dock my pay. It is not an inconvenience for me to buzz over to the health food store, and if I want to have mail-order food sent to me, I am at home to receive it.

There are few things more depressing to a working parent than to have to worry that her or his growing child's food source may be contaminated. Every study or front-page item on this subject throws parents into fits of despair. Tell a working mother that she ought to find organic food for her child, and that mother's face will show you what desolation really means. There is simply no time and often not enough money. Our present government (I am writing in October before the election of 1992) has done nothing to help us. As Ralph Nader has pointed out, we are allowing our children to be fed by large corporations who do not have our children's interests at heart.

I think we must lean on our government to protect us from agribusiness.

Furthermore, we have had a president publicly announce that he loathed broccoli, for which, if for no other reason, he should have been put out of office at once. Underneath this supposedly amusing confession was an utter insensitivity to children who might like broccoli and parents trying to get those kids to eat it if the head of their nation hadn't told them it was okay not to. Worst of all, most parents have to cope with television, which does almost nothing but beam into the extremely trusting brains of children what they ought to eat.

We do not have a television, but my daughter has a bash at one every now and again. She once came to me, her face awash with concern, and said, "Mom, I don't want you to make soup anymore." I asked her why she felt that way. She said, "Because it says on the television that Campbell's is better than homemade." This, I felt, was a dire indication of what's out there in television land.

The underlying reality here is that for all our food processors and fancy foods stores, our connection with food is really very low. We eat breakfast on the run. Our children's lunch boxes are filled with instant pudding, instant soup, peanut butter and jelly on packaged bread. Very often our evening meal comes from a package.

I do not believe that delicious food is a frill. I do not believe that putting dinner on the table should be the job of a usually very tired woman who has worked all day. We have to get our sons into the kitchen with us and teach them how to cook so that as adults our daughters do not end up working to a frazzle while our sons sit around reading the newspaper.

If we don't know how to cook—I mean *men* and women—we should learn how. Real men may not eat quiche, but there is nothing more attractive than a man who knows his way around the kitchen without making a huge production of it.

And we must not make assumptions about what children eat. They will eat anything if it is good. We must also realize that in some ways, they are *not* like us. Their taste buds are developing in a way we can't imagine and science can't deduce. Therefore a lovely plate of *ratatouille* may look extremely enticing to a toddler (especially if it is on *your* plate,) and that toddler may crawl on your lap and finish it off for you, but offer him or her a plate of it for lunch and you will be met with a look of sheer outrage. Some children like spicy food (to your amazement) one day and shun it the next. Like us they have crazes. They are experimental. I will never forget the look of rapture that crossed my daughter's face at her first taste of steamed zucchini. I myself hadn't eaten an un-adorned vegetable in years, so I tried some, realizing at once how delicious things are plain. It occurred to me that to their pure, unadulterated palates, things taste more intense, which explains to me why children seem to like things one at a time (the squash here, the bread here, the noodles there) than combinations such as lasagne. The exception to this appears to be soup.

It is also clear that children make a distinction between what they will eat at home and what they will eat out.

I once watched with avid interest as a classmate of my daughter's, a child whose mother said he had been living on hot dogs and his sister's baby food, happily scarfed down a large order of *moo shu* pork, which contains among other things tree ears (a ge-latinous Chinese fungus), bamboo shoots, and baby corn, none of which he would ever have touched at home. Home is full of prejudices, and rules, but a restaurant is not. It is, in fact, amazing what children will eat if they are given the chance.

I am the parent of an omnivore. She is the daughter of two people who like to eat, who take pleasure in food. One of her parents loves to cook. The other is happy to provision first-rate bread—being European, her father takes bread very seriously.

Like publishing companies and magazines, households have house styles. You child will probably eat what you like to give him or her. If you like fried okra and think it's swell, your child proba-bly will, too. I myself have converted many people who think they hate okra into okra lovers. But I have noticed that children pick up even the remotest bat squeak from parents concerning The Big Issues, one of which is food. Like love and money, food can be encrusted with all manner of other things.

For instance, I have a friend for whom family dinner is a sacred obligation. She comes home from work and prepares an old-fashioned dinner. This ritual makes her *feel* a certain way, but it does not make her child feel a certain way. The more the mother wants a confirming reaction from her child, the less her child is inclined to eat. There are, naturally, evenings when this child chows down like a horse (and the mother is a very good cook), but there are times when her hunger and her mother's need for stability in an artifact called mealtime do not jibe. The child's reluctance is seen as a play for power by a mother yearning for what she considers an appropriate response from her child.

I have another friend who is in fact a marvelous cook, but the burden of cooking, shopping, and planning is a chore (every cooking mother in the world has felt this way) and a bore and a dreaded obligation. She herself often forgets to eat, and her own attitudes about food are complicated at best. Her child, who is fearless in most other ways, is a reluctant eater.

When you think about what messages you are sending your child you must always remember the messages that were sent to you. We have all been brainwashed into believing that a proper diet consists of one starch or grain, some protein, and some vegetable. Almost any Asian above a certain income level would look at our tables in astonishment—at how impoverished our diet is. Any Indian, Korean, Japanese, or Chinese meal contains a number of dishes of vegetables and meat or fish, plus noodles, rice, and something pickled. Our tables still feature the large piece of meat, the potato, and some vegetables, which are very much an afterthought. What would happen if the vegetables were the first thought?

Because I am a crank, and because I was brought up by a family who found food interesting, entertaining, and valuable as well as necessary and sustaining, I took my child as a small person to the greenmarket with me when I shopped. There we encountered such things as zucchini blossoms, which, when fried in batter, were a great success. We discovered something called minaret broccoli or broccoli *romanesco,* also a hit. We bought quail eggs (very successful) and infinite varieties of apples (Arkansas black twig and mutsus are the two favorites).

What I was doing with my daughter was what was done with me. I was taken into the world of food—to the poultry lady who sold chickens and guinea hens, to the fish market, out crabbing for blue crabs. I have passed on to my daughter what was given to me: a sense of pleasure and delight in the bounty of the table.

And so if you want to feed your tot, my extreme advice is to take your television set and drive it to the dump or put it out on the street. Everyone in your family will profit from this, and you will not be driven insane in the supermarket by small people trying to bug you into buying piles of additive-filled junk.

Encourage your child to try everything. Make one family meal a week. If you are a single parent, invite some friends and tell them to bring something. Or invite yourself and your family to the home of someone who works at home and makes Friday night supper (*you* bring something). Take your child to the farm stand, the greenmarket, the produce section of the supermarket. Get your child into the kitchen with you if you cook. If you don't, acquire a nice, user-friendly cookbook (*Joy of Cooking* is everyone's friend) and learn to cook with your child. Try some appealing new thing as often as possible. Don't obsess about health. Ask your child's opinion and solicit his or her advice.

Food is not fuel. It is not nutrition. It is fun, educational, horizon expanding, delightful. It is consoling, transporting, and a comfort. If you want a happy eater, run a happy kitchen. These things take time, but so do all good things. Rejoice in what you have, be it rice and beans or baked Alaska. Be charmed by vegetables, and your child will be charmed, too. The fact is, if it is delicious, there is a good chance children will eat it.

We want our children to be independent thinkers, happy sweethearts, and cheerful parents, and it is not too much to ask that they be cheerful cooks and eaters, too.

In Search of Latvian Bread

When our daughter was born, my husband's oldest friend turned up with the perfect present: two loaves of sour Latvian rye bread. My husband was born in Latvia, as was his oldest friend. I stared at this loaf—a large, shiny, dark, mahogany-colored rectangle—and wondered what it was I had married into. The bread was cut. I took a bite. It was so sour I blinked, but by the second bite I was hooked. Besides being delicious, it was *fortifying,* and was, in fact, a very useful baby present—that is, useful to the baby's exhausted parents.

It turned out that the ninety-year-old woman who had come from Latvia some years ago with her bread trough and baked bread each week at the Latvian church had taken her bread trough and gone back to Riga. After the last scrap of bread was eaten, my husband was bereft. "Never mind," I said. "I'm an ace bread baker. I'll bake you some. Call your mother."

He called his mother. A long conversation in a language I do not speak (Lettish) ensued. An hour later my husband handed me a sheaf of papers. I rifled through them.

"Day one," I read. "Day two. Day three. Hey!" I said. "This bread takes *three days*."

"Never mind," said my husband. "We'll do it on vacation. I'll help."

That was quite a few years ago. In the meanwhile, I was recently given a jar of eleven-year-old sourdough starter, another of those perfect presents one finds oneself staring at. It looked like batter and smelled like library paste.

I have been reading about sourdough starters for years, but frankly, I was too chicken to start one. I never took chemistry in high school, and besides, even if by some miracle it came out right, sourdough starters sounded demanding—what with stirring them or using them once a week and taking them out for an airing and keeping them in the right place in the fridge. With a small child around, I said to myself, who needs a sourdough starter? You might as well get a dog.

But there it was, safe in my fridge, and on my desk was a brief note about its use (keep it in the fridge and replenish as used) and a nice recipe for sourdough bread.

This bread called for starter and yeast. It made a very good loaf, and, according to my book on science in the kitchen, bread made with sourdough starter has a lower pH—or is it higher? I was never very good at these things. However, it wasn't sour.

My family craves sour bread, and I find myself bringing examples of it home whenever I can. Recently my daughter told me that she wanted her sandwiches on *miche,* a whole-wheat sourdough bread made by a company called Bread Alone, which drives a truck from Boiceville, New York, to my local green-market.

One day it occurred to me that I might take a bash at real sourdough bread myself. After all, didn't I have an eleven-year-old starter in my fridge?

Day one: I mixed 1 cup of sourdough starter, 2 cups of whole-wheat flour, and 2 cups of water, creating a sloppy batter that smelled of library paste.

Day two: The batter was bubbling nicely. Smelling very sour—a *clean* sour smell. I added 2 more cups of whole-wheat flour, salt, and water and stirred it up.

Day three: I added 2 more cups of flour, kneaded the dough, and let it sit all day in a cool place.

Day three, afternoon: I punched the dough down, formed two loaves, and baked.

The results, to my mind, were mixed. An Estonian came for supper and said it tasted exactly like the bread he had had in Moscow. I was not sure that this was a compliment. A dancer friend, also at dinner, tasted it and said he liked the other bread (*miche* from the greenmarket) better. My husband said that it was wonderful, but that I should have added rye flour. The Estonian said this bread would keep forever. I was not sure that this was a compliment.

I mentally contrasted it to true Latvian bread, which is dense and robust. Its sourness verges on sweetness, and the texture is satiny. It is certainly the best bread I have ever had. It is unlikely that I will replicate it in my own home (although I am sure I will come up with something sort of like it). After all, I do not have a ninety-year-old bread trough, and my starter is a mere child. Instructions in various old books instruct never to wash the bread bowl, as bits of the dough provide leavening for the next batch; they also encourage the use of a wooden bread bowl, which I don't have.

As for my starter, it lives in a big former peanut butter jar. It used to have a paper label, but that has shredded off. The jar itself is festooned with dried drips of starter. After a while the dough and the water separate slightly, not a beautiful sight. But when I open the fridge, it crosses my mind that there's something *alive* in there.

So now I have my work cut out for me. When we go away for a month in the country we will pack ourselves, our cat, and our sourdough starter. I will acquire organic rye flour, and in the tranquility of our rustic setting, I will attempt real Latvian sour rye. My landlady in the country has nothing suitable for a bread bowl, but we can't let these little things stand in our way.

And if all else fails, my husband has tracked down a one-man Latvian home bakery in Bolton, Connecticut—Juris Kupris Home Bakery, who sells his bread mail-order, just in case.

Butter

Years and years and years ago, when people still served rib roast without batting an eye and before the surgeon general had determined that cigarettes were bad for you, my mother would make butter balls. She took very cold pats of butter and rolled them between two flat, ridged wooden paddles that had been chilled in the freezer beforehand—these paddles used to appear before dinner parties to fancy up the butter—working them until they became little balls, with crosshatched surfaces. Then, she made a hole in each ball, sprinkled in a pinch of sugar and a drop of lemon juice, and put the balls in the fridge. Later, my sister and I were allowed to eat the butter balls as a treat, and, believe me, they were wonderful.

There is nothing like butter. As Harold McGee, author of *On Food and Cooking: The Science and Lore of the Kitchen*, says, it is a sauce in itself and needs no embellishments. I cannot think of anything butter does not render more delicious, and I have never met anyone who doesn't love butter, although many people have given it up for reasons of health.

Unfortunately, no substitute for its exists. Father Robert Farrar

Capon, in his noble book *The Supper of the Lamb*, suggests that, if you are going to refrain from butter, you ought not con yourself into accepting some nasty imitation. He feels people ought to use good-quality olive oil and, once in a while, allow a measure of real, true, pure butter. This is extremely sensible advice.

There are, as we know, two kinds of butter: salted and sweet. The salted is a hangover from the days before refrigeration, when people salted their butter to keep it from going bad, and it is now part of the American palate. I myself prefer sweet, and, even in the days when I was a salt addict, I used to spread my bread with sweet butter and sprinkle salt on top. When people asked why I didn't simply buy salted butter, I pointed out that sweet butter—even with a little salt on top—has a totally different flavor. Semolina bread, sweet butter, and a little sea salt is a combination I would happily walk over hot coals for.

There is also something called "whipped" butter, a substance I have never understood unless one likes a quantity of air in one's food. Apparently this stuff spreads better, but I am of the school that, except in the dog days of summer, believes in leaving butter out. I hate to put it in the fridge, where it often becomes what my mother used to call "ice-boxy." If you leave it out, it stays nice and spreadable; furthermore, it is my belief that the taste of things at room temperature is their true taste.

Luckily, you can find ways around a life without butter. Place by your night table some books on Mediterranean or Chinese cooking, two of the many cuisines that do not use butter. Make sure the bread you buy is sensational: Really good bread needs nothing at all, which comes as a shock to people who feel that a piece of bread is the mere vehicle for a large slab of butter. If you don't live near a wonderful bakery, find one from which to mail-order, or take up baking. You can buy or make some really wonderful jam and some first-rate organic peanut butter. You might also treat yourself to a bottle of rich, green, fruity extra-virgin olive oil.

You can sauté your string beans in dark sesame oil and drizzle that lovely olive oil on your broccoli, and you can take comfort from the fact that you do not have to dip your artichoke leaves in melted butter but can eat them perfectly plain. You will also come to see that melted butter with lobster is just plain decadent.

It is always instructive to do without. A naked baked russet or sweet potato will show you how wonderful these things are by themselves. An unadorned vegetable—a truly fresh vegetable, nicely steamed—is simply full of itself.

After you have been a very good person for a very long time and are thin as a bean, you may decide to fall briefly into sin. You will want something simple and elegant that cannot be made without butter. There is only one thing that will do: shortbread.

I would rather eat shortbread than any cake or cookie in the world. I would turn my back on a chocolate truffle or a banana split for one piece of crisp, melting shortbread. It is the essence of butter. Although you can fancy shortbread up by serving it with vanilla ice cream or turning it into cookies with raspberry jam or messing around and putting toasted walnuts or ginger in it—the pure, plain thing is a wonder in itself. A child can make it, and often shortbread is the first thing children learn to bake.

Classic Shortbread

1. Cream 1 stick of butter with ¼ cup confectioners' (powdered) sugar. Add ½ teaspoon vanilla.
2. Work in ¾ cup all-purpose flour sifted with ¼ cup rice flour, ⅛ teaspoon baking powder, and ⅛ teaspoon salt. (Classic Scottish recipes use rice flour to give the short-bread a slightly grainy crispness that is very delicious. You can find rice flour at specialty foods shops and natural foods stores. However, if an extra stop is not on your shopping agenda, you may eliminate the rice flour and use 1 cup all-purpose flour.)
3. Pat the dough into an 8-inch circle on an ungreased cookie sheet. This recipe gives you a very soft, delicate dough, so be patient with it. Before baking, score the dough, making 6 wedges, and mark the edge with the tines of a fork.
4. Bake the shortbread in a preheated 375° F. oven for about 20 minutes, or until the edge is golden brown.
5. While the shortbread is still warm, cut it into the wedges with a sharp knife.

There you have it. A true, no-fault, idiot-proof dessert, beloved by adults and children (animals often go for it, too). And once a year, as a special reward, there is no better use for a quarter pound of butter.

Desserts That Quiver

One day a friend who was going to China for a year cleaned out her pantry and gave my daughter and me a present, an instant gelatin dessert she said her children had always loved. It came in a little box with a picture on the front showing a three-layered concoction in a fancy glass. Inside the package was a poisonous-looking green powder that smelled like artificially flavored lime cough syrup. To this you added first hot water and then cold water, then you beat the mixture, then you did something else to it that I can't remember, and then you put it in the fridge in little glasses.

The result was three loathsome layers: The bottom was a plain gelatin but of a sort resembling a sweet you can buy for children in a small plastic trash can and that is called Green Slime. The second layer was a spongy green stuff, and the third layer looked like a decrepit form of meringue. This was referred to as "chiffon."

My daughter was enraptured, and she gamely attempted to eat the dish, although it was clearly an effort. She asked me to try it, with a puzzled look on her face. It tasted exactly like an English cough preparation called Lucozade, and I could not imagine why anyone would want to eat it. But my daughter was crushed.

It looked so pretty and she did so want to like it that I set out to make a gelatin dessert we all could stand.

The solution was ridiculously obvious: fruit juice and unflavored gelatin. The recipe on the box of unflavored gelatin suggested 1 envelope of gelatin to 2 cups fruit juice, and so I went on a search mission to my local health food store to see what they had in the way of exotic, organic fruit juices. I found thousands. I made gels out of watermelon, blackberry, and peach juices, as well as lingonberry, apricot, and grape. These were all successful, and so I decided to gild the lily and load them up with fruit.

At that moment all I had in the house were some kumquats, which I sliced up and put in the bottom of a number of custard cups. These cups had sat on a shelf for years gathering dust, causing my husband to wonder why I kept them. As soon as our daughter was two he stopped asking, because it became clear that custard cups are extremely useful to have around if you have a small child. Besides, they are pretty. On top of the kumquats I put lemonade-flavored gelatin, a towering success. Eventually I went on to make dozens of combinations, always at the spur of the moment: apple cider gel with raisins and apples, pear with raspberries, lemon with sour cherries—the list went on and on. Amazingly enough, it turned out that adults liked these as well. They are not too sweet, very refreshing, and good for you.

Next I set out to find some gelatin desserts that a person might serve at a dinner party. I wanted to go beyond Bavarian cream, which is a nice enough dessert but rather dull. In Jane Grigson's sacred tome, *Good Things,* I found what I was looking for. Jane Grigson was never as famous in this country as she ought to have been. I simply could not do without her books, all filled with inspiring prose, plain, elegant recipes, and sound advice. If I were allowed only one cookbook, *Good Things* by Jane Grigson would be it. One reason is that it contains a recipe for "honeycomb mould," the three-layered dessert of my daughter's dreams.

Of this splendid dish Mrs. Grigson writes: "This delicious pudding of childhood should not be relegated to the nursery. Its clear, true flavour (not to be found in the packet-mix versions) is a luxury these days." It is a wonderful dessert and quite easy to make. If you have an ornamental mold, use it.

Honeycomb Mould After Jane Grigson
(Three-Layered Lemon Gel)

1. Separate the yolks and whites of 3 large eggs.
2. Put the yolks in a metal bowl and whisk in ¾ teaspoon freshly grated lemon zest, a ¼-ounce envelope of unflavored gelatin, ½ cup sugar, and ⅓ cup heavy cream.
3. Heat 1½ cups milk (or half-and-half) to just under boiling and whisk it gradually into the egg yolks. Set the bowl over a pan of simmering water (or you can do this in a double boiler) and stir the mixture until you have a thin custard. (For health reasons, the custard should be cooked until it reaches 175° F. on a candy thermometer.)
4. Mix in the strained juice of 2 lemons (about 6 tablespoons). Working quickly, beat the egg whites until they are stiff and fold them into the hot custard. (Mrs. Grigson recommends the use of a metal spoon rather than

a wooden one for folding: I have used a rubber spatula, which works fine, too.)

5. Let the mixture stand for 4 minutes.
6. Pour the mixture into a 1-quart mold or bowl and chill it, covered, overnight. Run a knife around the edge of the pudding, dip the mold in warm water for 10 seconds, and turn the pudding out onto a plate.

In Mrs. Grigson's words: "[The dessert] will have a cap of clear lemon jelly, then a thin band of opaque cream jelly shading off a honeycombed spongy base which makes a slight crinkling noise as it's eaten."

This is not something to feed to the cholesterol-conscious crowd, but it is the three-layered pudding that people long for, even if they have never seen one before. Its flavor *is* clear and true, and it is fun to eat.

My other great gelatin dessert comes from that mighty American cookbook *The Taste of Country Cooking* by Edna Lewis. This is the second cookbook I would choose if I could have only two. It is a treasure and deserves to be in every American house. Mrs. Lewis calls this dish *blancmange,* but it is a variation of an old, old American pudding (formerly an old English pudding) made with almonds.

Blancmange After Edna Lewis

1. Drop 1 cup almonds with skins into boiling water and let them stand for a few minutes off the heat. The almonds will then slip easily out of their skins.

2. Put the skinned almonds, about ¼ cup at a time, into a blender with ⅓ cup cold water each time (you will use 1⅓ cups water altogether) and grind the mixture until it is smooth. Transfer each batch to a bowl to make room for the next, but put everything back into the blender at the end and blend the purée one more time until it is as smooth as possible.

3. In a bowl combine ½ cup milk, ½ cup heavy cream, and ⅔ cup sugar (or less, to your taste; I use a *very* scant ⅔ cup). Add this to the almond purée, blend the mixture well, and strain it in batches through a very fine sieve into a bowl. Strain the mixture in batches again into a saucepan. (Again, smoothness is the aim: Don't press on the solids as you go, and discard them between batches.) There should be about 2 cups.

4. Dissolve 1 tablespoon unflavored gelatin in ¼ cup cold water, add the mixture to the pan, and heat the mixture to just under boiling. Stir in ¼ teaspoon almond extract and 1 teaspoon vanilla, pour the pudding into a 2-cup mold, and chill it, covered, overnight. Run a knife around the edge of the pudding, dip the mold in warm water for 10 seconds, and turn the pudding out onto a plate. Serve the pudding with fresh raspberries.

This *blancmange* will change forever the way you feel about anything made with gelatin. It is sublime. Besides, there are few things nicer or more convenient than a dessert that is child- and adult-friendly at the same time.

Rented-House Cookery

There is something liberating about cooking in a rented house. Suddenly your daily props are gone, and you are in unfamiliar territory. Terrifying as this sometimes is, it is always good for you. Cooking in the summer is like nothing else, and cooking in the summer in a rented house is rather like taking off your winter underwear and putting on a filmy pinafore. You feel light and strange, and interesting things occur to you.

The first house I ever rented was off the coast of Maine, a little Cape Cod house with a deck, an electric stove (I had never used one of these before), and almost no kitchen equipment of any kind. I was also unused to an oven, having spent eight years cooking on what amounted to a hot plate, but I was game. I remember that we mostly ate lobster out. It was cheap, and I was scared. We ate eggs and toasted cheese, and had big breakfasts, after which we placed dots of bread on the deck rails and watched the same sea gull come day after day to eat it.

One afternoon I opened up my copy of *Joy of Cooking* and decided to make custard, which instantly curdled. I was instructed to beat it vigorously with a whisk, but this rented house had no whisk. Instead it had one of those little contraptions with a spring on it that bartenders use to make drinks with egg whites. This inefficient tool was no help at all, and I remember flinging the pot into the sink and flouncing out of the house in tears, which I wept bitterly in a pine wood surrounded by *clavaria* and Indian pipes.

As I gained confidence in the kitchen I got the hang of cooking in rented houses. I took along my favorite knife, a knife sharpener, and a wonderful cookbook entitled *The Four Seasons' Cookery Book* by Margaret Costa, unavailable in this country for reasons I have never understood. Heavily in use most of the year, this book comes away every summer and sits acquiring a thin layer of cobwebbing. What I have learned is that in summer you don't have to cook—you let the food do the work.

A sharp knife and a supply of tomatoes is all one needs to make tomato salad. Add some fried bread and you have a first course. Offer some corn on the cob, a plate of steamed vegetables, and some homemade mayonnaise if you have the energy. For dessert, peaches, berries, and melons in their natural state without a thing on them. After a day of water and sunshine people are hungry, but no one wants to fuss, and since on vacation all plans go to hell, no one feels guilty about sandwiches for supper.

In rented houses I cook things I never cook at home. I make meat loaf and turn the remains into casseroles with noodles and eggplant. I roast a chicken in the morning, stick it in the fridge, and have it cold for supper. I make baked eggs with toast and corn pudding.

But all rented houses pale in comparison with our rented farmhouse in Minorca. Ten years ago three couples decided to rent a farmhouse on this peaceful Balearic island. Our house was of a kind of adobe with tiled floors. Our terrace abounded in hedgehogs at night, and during the day immense black bees, known to us as B-52s, buzzed around the bougainvillea. In the morning, since I was the first one up, I would make the coffee and then pick the last apricots off the tree and bring them to my husband for breakfast. Then we went into town to shop.

The bread was white bread, except for something known as an invalid loaf, a kind of whole-wheat *baguette.* We would buy a bag full, and kilos of tomatoes and onions, and a wonderful, very cowy cheese that came in the shape of a square. The older it got, the more it was like Parmesan, but you could buy it in any stage of its life. We bought an entire cheese and kept it under glass in the kitchen. Then we bought fish and went home to make lunch.

Lunch was taken at the beach—beautiful white Mediterranean beaches. We packed our wicker basket with onion, tomato, and cheese sandwiches dripping with olive oil. My husband ate these by the dozens. I do not think he would have eaten them at home. We packed rice salads and vegetables, and off we went. Once we had polished off our lunch and felt the need for a little something, we went to the beach kiosk for potato *frittatas,* which I make to this day, and café con leche. Then it was time for dinner.

There were usually four of us in the kitchen, preparing salad, bread, cheese, *ratatouille,* and fish. One afternoon we spent hours stuffing squid, which we cooked in milk. This was not delicious, so we cut it up, put it in an earthenware bowl, and fed it to the stray cats that lived in a cactus thicket by an old stone wall.

The next morning we were off again to buy almonds (which we fried in olive oil and salted) and more cheese and more bread, and then to the beach and then out to dinner.

We cooked shrimp fried in garlic and butter, and we stewed fava beans and ate *mel e motto*—new cheese, honey, and toasted hazelnuts. Then we bought our own oval wicker picnic baskets, our sandals made of rubber tires, and our huge earthenware dishes that can be used on top of the stove and went home to feed our friends Minorcan potatoes all winter long.

Northwestern Connecticut is considerably less exotic, but summer is itself exotic. In our rented house in Connecticut I can wash the dishes and watch hummingbirds drinking nectar from the rose of Sharon trees.

Tomatoes

There are very few things mankind cannot live without. For centuries we survived without compact discs, automated bank tellers, iceberg lettuce, and bubble gum–flavored toothpaste, to say nothing of the internal combustion engine.

But life as we know it would be unimaginable without the tomato: Half of our soups, pasta sauces, and pizzas would vanish. No gazpacho, no ketchup. Our stews would lose their snap; our chili would fall flat. Every time you turn around, the tomato is giving its wonderful flavor to something. How empty our grocery shelves would be without puréed tomatoes, *pomodori pelati,* tomato paste in cans and tubes, sun-dried tomatoes, tomato soup, tomato juice, and the imported crushed tomatoes that come in those little boxes!

One of the joys of summer is to go roaming through the garden, pulling ripe tomatoes off the vine and biting in. Juice and seeds drip all over your nice white shirt, but who cares? In summer the idea is to eat as many tomatoes as you can and enjoy the luxury of getting sick of them. When September rolls around, they have become a little woolly and somewhat less flavorsome. Then it is time to lay in a big supply of canned tomatoes—store-bought or homemade—to take you through the winter. A world without tomatoes is like a string quartet without violins.

My own idea of pure bliss is the tomato sandwich, which is good on any kind of bread, from grainy imported *vollkornbrot* to suave, textureless semolina. This sandwich can only be made with ripe tomatoes, luscious and full of seeds. The bread is slathered with mayonnaise, then dusted with celery salt and layered with thinly sliced tomatoes. I prefer this sandwich open, but it is fine with a lid.

My favorite salad is the ubiquitous salad of the Middle East: diced cucumber, onion, and tomato dressed with salt, pepper, olive oil, and lemon juice. If you fry up some squares of *pita* bread in olive oil and add some flat-leafed parsley and a little fresh mint, you have a salad called *fattosh,* which is ridiculously delicious and extremely simple to make. This salad, with or without bread, is my summer staple. I often make a large batch, eat it all for lunch myself, and then have to compose another batch for dinner.

The tomato, summer and winter, is everyone's friend. The world's easiest and quickest pasta sauce can be made with fresh tomatoes, cherry tomatoes, or drained canned tomatoes, which you dice and sauté in olive oil with minced garlic and hot red pepper flakes. This takes under ten minutes and always tastes good. With freshly grated cheese, you can't ask for anything better.

I have never yet encountered tomatoes in any form unloved by me. Often at night I find myself ruminating about two previously mysterious tomato dishes, which I was brazen enough to get the recipes for. One is Tomato Pie and is a staple of a tea shop called Chaiwalla, owned by Mary O'Brien, in Salisbury, Connecticut. According to Mary, the original recipe was found in a cookbook put out by the nearby Hotchkiss School, but she has changed it sufficiently to claim it as her own. The pie has a double biscuit-dough crust, made by blending 2 cups flour, 1 stick butter, 4 teaspoons baking powder, and approximately ¾ cup milk, either by hand or in a food processor. You roll out half the dough on a floured surface and line a 9-inch pie plate with it. Then you add the tomatoes. Mary makes this pie year round and uses first-quality canned tomatoes, but at this time of year 2 pounds peeled fresh tomatoes are fine, too. Drain well and slice thin two 28-ounce cans plum tomatoes, then lay the slices over the crust and scatter them with chopped basil, chives, or scallions, depending on their availability and your mood. Grate 1½ cups sharp Cheddar and sprinkle 1 cup of it on top of the tomatoes. Then over this drizzle ⅓ cup mayonnaise that has been thinned with 2 tablespoons lemon juice, and top everything with the rest of the grated Cheddar. Roll out the remaining dough, fit it over the filling, and pinch the edges of the dough together to seal them. Cut several steam vents in the top crust and bake the pie at 400° F. for about 25 minutes. The secret of this pie, according to Mary, is to reheat it before serving, which among other things ensures that the cheese is soft and gooey. She usually bakes it early in the morning, then reheats it in the evening in a 350° F. oven until it is hot.

It is hard to describe how delicious this is, especially on a hot day with a glass of magnificent iced tea in a beautiful setting, but it would doubtless be just as scrumptious on a cold day in your warm kitchen with a cup of coffee.

The other tomato concoction has no name. I had it at a very fancy buffet as a side dish . . . or condiment. . . . Whatever it was, I tried not to disgrace myself by eating enormous quantities of it, but I was not successful. I could not get enough. Finally I snagged a waiter and begged him to tell me what it was.

Apparently you take numerous cans of plum tomatoes, drain the tomatoes, put them into a large roasting pan, drizzle them with olive oil, and sprinkle them with chopped garlic. You then bake this in a moderate oven for a very long time—the waiter was unclear about how long, but he did say you had to stir it once every half hour to get the browned parts mixed in with the rest. This might be a good thing to try on a winter's day when you have no intention of leaving the house and have invited a couple of worthy friends to come for dinner. It would also be heaven on a wet summer evening, served hot or cold. With a loaf of bread and a bean salad, this makes a dinner I would walk through fire for.

My daughter has a book titled *Little Dog Dreaming,* the story of a city dog who gets to go to the country for the summer and spends the winter lying on various chairs and sofas dreaming and dreaming about the exact spot in which he has buried his bone.

I spend my winter daydreaming about the exact bowl I am going to make my first summer tomato salad in and about how I will not feel the slightest twinge of remorse if I buy the last two bags of tomatoes at the organic farm stand (a nicer person would leave a bag for someone else). I have been known to open one of these bags in the car and eat most of it *without sharing* on the way home. These are the sorts of deep, primitive feelings inspired by tomatoes, and I am convinced that there are millions of citizens out there just like me.

On one of the great days of my life, a friend with an enormous garden invited me and a pal to wander through his tomato patch and take as many plump specimens as we wanted; it was the end of the summer, and he had overplanted. I felt like the person in the Andrew Marvell poem "The Garden," about whose head ripe apples fall, except that these were tomatoes—in this case sharp, ripe, juicy cherry tomatoes.

In this world of uncertainty and woe, one thing remains unchanged: Fresh, canned, puréed, dried, salted, sliced, and served with sugar and cream, or pressed into juice, the tomato is reliable, friendly, and delicious. We would be nothing without it.

Picnics

Many years ago I took a stand against picnics. When dragged into the out-of-doors for lunch I would crab about sand in my food, yellow jackets buzzing near my drink, and itchy wool blankets that did not protect my tender flesh from lumpy, damp, uneven ground. Furthermore I hate sitting out in the sun, and I found most picnic food boring.

The picnics that appealed to me were the sort no one ever invited me to—the kind described in Jennifer Brennan's wonderful book *Curries and Bugles: A Memoir and a Cookbook of the British Raj,* in which parties of servants carried exotic things up mountainsides and cooked over portable stoves. Or those fancy tailgate picnics that you used to see in glossy, sophisticated magazines: the gleaming Rolls-Royce, the perfectly equipped wicker hamper, the cold pheasant, the selection of pâtés and cheeses, the Champagne bucket, the real china, and white linen napkins.

Instead I often found myself balancing a tippy paper plate containing a sandwich that had not yet fallen into an anthill, my napkin blown away in the wind, my glass infested by stinging insects, and I sunburnt, peeling, and in a bad mood.

I said that if I had to endure eating outside I would prefer a screened-in porch, but these do not abound in nature. So I trekked along, complaining under my breath and wishing for a better life.

Then my husband and I, along with two other couples, rented a farmhouse on the island of Minorca, a Balearic island off the coast of Barcelona, and there I changed my attitude.

We were squired around the island by a picnic-loving American girl who had spent her teen years on Minorca and was happy to show it off to a bunch of tourists. In order to sightsee and swim, you had to pack a lunch.

And so we piled into her car, the trunk filled with baskets of every shape, and went off to find lovely beachy spots, with lots of sun, lots of shade, and perfect swimming.

Although this experience liberated me from the notion that a picnic need feature little more than sandwiches, it remains true that there is no real picnic without them. The bread we found on Minorca was the sort made to be a sponge for sopping up sauces, and it tasted rather like sponge but resembled large versions of those tiny plaster loaves you find in dollhouse stores. If you left them out on the counter for too long, they took on the texture of a plaster loaf and were no good at all.

Our guide took us to a bakery that made something called "invalid bread," which was said to be fortifying to sick people. We bought dozens of these whole-wheat *baguettes,* split them, sprinkled them with olive oil, and loaded them up with Mahón cheese, sweet onion, and tomato. Hands down they were the best sandwiches I have ever eaten.

And then we packed everything else that was lying around: leftover squid, rice salad, cold potato *frittata.* The idea was (and still is) that a picnic can be anything. It can resemble the Mad

Hatter's tea party if you want it to. Its heart and soul is breeziness, invention, and enough to eat for people made ravenous by fresh air.

As there were no paper plates or plastic forks, we packed the real thing and hauled pottery bowls, wheels of cheese, and cutting boards up and down hills. When all had been consumed, we dove into the clear green water and splashed around for hours.

One memorable day we gathered ourselves into our trusty guide's car. We were going to the loveliest and most remote beach on the island, we were told. Our guide had never been there. It would be a long, long car trip, but the view was said to be spectacular, the beach empty and beautiful, the water pristine.

And so we drove and drove down an endless, dusty, isolated dirt road. We passed one lonely farmhouse in front of which hunting dogs were chained. We continued to drive. It seemed to us that we might do so for the rest of our lives, and we were starved. Finally we saw the gleam of green water. We began a downhill drive toward the beach, at the bottom of which were hundreds of girl scouts, their tents pitched, having a camp-out. They were not at all pleased to see us.

Of course, a vacation on Minorca is a dream and in no way resembles real life, which is usually everything a holiday is not: harried, pressured, and often without inspiration. But a picnic can be rather like a dream if you pick your spot, your companions, and your food. You can make it as simple or elaborate as you want.

My friend Cynthia B. Elitzer, mother of three and an ace cook, is of the throw-it-in-the-picnic-basket (hers is a large Portuguese market one) and compose-it-*in-situ* school. You pack a knife, a hard salami, some cheese, a loaf of bread, and a cutting board and make your sandwiches when you want them. A precomposed sandwich is a soggy sandwich—this is Cynthia's motto. It is impossible to have a picnic in her company without tasting some of the pasta salad she makes exclusively for these occasions. The salad contains *penne,* chopped Italian parsley, fresh basil, black pepper, and kidney beans that have been marinated overnight in a vinaigrette. Small children love this and eat large platefuls.

I myself rather like a soggy sandwich, and I make a few more than I need so that, for variety's sake, I can swap a few for someone else's sandwiches. I also feel in my heart of hearts that a picnic is an excuse to buy an enormous bag of potato chips and eat lots and lots of them. And I think that leftovers make interesting additions to any picnic. My particular favorite in this department is cold chicken, and my favorite preparation is what might be called Fake Tandoori Chicken. It is not authentic anything, but it is extremely simple and very delicious hot, cold, or lukewarm.

For one cut-up chicken—with or without skin, either way is fine—you need an 8-ounce container of plain yogurt (though you may not use all of it). What you want to make is a paste of yogurt, chili powder, and sweet paprika. The proportions are up to you, depending on how spicy you like your food; I personally use 2 tablespoons chili powder and 1 tablespoon paprika. Into the paste you grate or press a garlic clove. Paint the chicken all over with this paste and keep it, covered, in the fridge all day. Then bake the chicken in a pan lined with foil at 400° F. for 50 minutes to an hour, or until it is the color of teak. With the skin on it's crispy; off, it's crunchy. (You may have to pour off the juices halfway through the cooking time.) The yogurt, a natural tenderizer, gives the chicken an amazingly velvety texture and calms down the chili powder. I love this chicken and would eat it every other day if my family would let me. It makes absolutely splendid picnic fare.

The proper attitude toward a picnic is somewhat devil-may-care. You do not have to stand in the kitchen cutting perfect sandwiches and making perfect potato salad or frying chicken (although every once in a while an old-fashioned picnic is just the thing). So what if all you have in the fridge is leftover rice, a couple of scallions, and a jar of almonds? You may have invented a lovely new rice salad, and no one will care if it is not their usual, because you are on a picnic.

Besides, if they hate your last-minute rice salad they may very well love your salami and cream cheese sandwiches or a piece of bread with a slice of Brie and some *arugula* on it. And, if they are still starving, you can generously feed them a few crumbs of potato chips, if you have any left.

Waiting for Dessert

It often seems that the world divides (evenly or unevenly) into those who are waiting for dessert and those who have to produce it.

As to the producers, they are often waiting around for some brilliant recipe to find its way to them, for as we all know, when you invite people for dinner, you have to give them something sweet. People who are pressed for time often get around this problem by shopping. Their theory is that a bought dessert is better than a bad dessert or no dessert. A perfect example of this can be found in the poet Randall Jarrell's only novel, the sublime *Pictures from an Institution*. The novelist Gertrude Johnson gives a dinner party of which the author says: "But her cooking was neither a Southern cook's nor a Northern cook's nor a cook's: it was the cooking of a child. There was very little of Gertrude's dinner, but what there was was awful." Naturally the guests greet with rapture the dessert bought at a nice bakery.

But some people feel that this is cheating: If they are going to the trouble of making dinner, they ought to go the distance and make dessert. After you have washed the lettuce, trussed the chicken, made the dressing, and chopped or peeled the vegetables, the dessert is the fun part.

And some people, like me, are looking for something easy. For the exhausted or fainthearted there is always fruit, which in itself is good. For example, a beautiful bunch of grapes. In the season, if you happen to have a little extra cash on hand, a beautiful bunch of Champagne grapes. For those who have never encountered them, these are tiny grapes the size and color of garnets and about as expensive. They are sweet, tender, and almost melt in your mouth. It is impressive to me to observe how many bunches of these small children can put away: After all, Champagne grapes are *little*, the perfect child food. In addition to their other qualities, they are like works of art and require of the host or hostess only a nice-looking plate to put them on.

For the slightly less exhausted, fruit salad, especially when fancied up with some drained canned lichees or crystallized ginger (or both) is always a hit and good for you, too. You can go so far as to make a little syrup to drip over fruit salads, but if you are too lazy, weight-conscious, or tired, a dish of sugar on the side (especially some nice, large-crystal sugar such as Demerara) is a festive touch.

People who feel they must make a real dessert are often looking for something simple and wonderful, two words often felt to be mutually exclusive.

I like a cake that takes about four seconds to put together and gives an ambrosial result. Fortunately, there are such cakes, and usually you get them at the homes of others. You then purloin the recipe (since you have taken care to acquire generous friends) and serve it to other friends, who then serve it to others. This is the way in which nations are unified and friendships made solid.

My candidate for an easy, spectacular dessert is something called Nantucket Cranberry Pie, which is not a pie, but a cake, and was served to me in the country by my friend Ann Gold, who lives on a dairy farm and got this recipe from her mother, who can no longer remember where it came from. It is a Gold family staple, and the buck stops there.

In an effort to find the true roots of this cake I looked into *Yankee Cooking* by Imogen Walcott, a classic tome that contains everything anyone needs to know about New England cooking. There in the index was Cape Cod Cranberry Pie, but this turned out to be a real live pie, whereas Nantucket Cranberry Pie is a cake. Furthermore, it is a *snap,* and, last but not least, it is truly good. If you wanted to do some lily-gilding, you might put some vanilla ice cream (or *crème fraîche* or, if you have tons of time, custard) on the side, but Ann Gold serves it straight, which is, I feel, the best way.

Nantucket Cranberry Pie

1. Chop enough cranberries to make 2 cups and enough walnuts to make ½ cup.
2. In the bottom of a 10-inch pie plate or springform pan, place chopped cranberries, chopped walnuts, and ½ cup sugar.

3. Mix 2 eggs, ¾ cup melted butter, 1 cup sugar, 1 cup flour, and 1 teaspoon almond extract. Stir till smooth.

4. Pour over cranberry-walnut mixture and bake for 40 minutes at 350° F.

Plums or peaches would probably work as well, but there is something about the tartness of the cranberries and the smooth, sweet, buttery taste of the cake that is irresistible. This cake is so easy a child could do it, and if you happen to have a child or two lying around, I suggest you set them to work for your next dinner party.

It has always been my feeling that, at the end of the day, what a person wants in the way of dessert is something consoling and uncomplicated. The cook wants that, too.

But what about summer? In summer no one wants to use the oven. Moreover people who have been commuting through the heat are exhausted. Or they have spent their day in a car full of children who then spill out onto the beach and have to be sun-blocked, desanded, prevented from splashing adults, and kept afloat. Or a person has been gardening. For these people, here is the most minimal of all desserts (besides a pear and a knife): Frozen Mango Purée.

This takes a tiny bit of work, one ingredient, and no heat. Purchase (for four people) 2 big, really ripe mangoes. Peel them, cut off the flesh, and mash it with a fork. Pack the pulp into custard cups or ramekin dishes, and stick it in the freezer.

If your freezer, like mine, is a dud, you needn't worry too much. Stir it from time to time. If you have a whizbang Zero

King, stir often and remove about 10 minutes before serving. You might want to fancy this up with a piece of candied ginger on the top or not. Mangoes are among the most delicious things in the world, and the fact that you have taken all the work out of eating them will make your guests know you truly care. And since you know in advance how happy they will be, you can tell *them* to bring the cookies.

How to Cook Like an American

There is nothing like a visitor from another continent to confuse you about your own homeland. One night an Indian friend came to dinner. He was a pleasure to feed because he was skinny and ate like a horse. As I have a fascination with Indian food, I cooked him an Indian dish and then begged for a critique, pelting him with questions about ingredients, presentation, and the authenticity of the recipe. But after the meal he turned the tables on me.

He asked me to help him figure out American cooking, at which point I drew a blank. He said: "I would like to cook some American dishes, but it is hard for me to tell just what American food *is*."

Of course it was doubly hard for him because he lives in New York City, where *hummus, sushi,* bagels, and jerk chicken are all considered standard fare.

I tried to put together a hypothetical meal for my Indian friend: fried chicken (which the Chinese have been cooking for thousands of years), gumbo (of African descent), coleslaw (from Germany), and strawberry shortcake (the basic element of which is either an English biscuit or an English spongecake). No wonder he was confused! I was pretty confused myself.

In anthropology courses we learn that a culture consists not merely of great artifacts and rituals but also of the ordinary things ordinary people use and do. With this thought in mind I defined American food for myself: *American food is what Americans eat.* Therefore it matters not one bit that hot dogs come from Frankfurt and hamburgers from Hamburg.

What my friend was really asking for was *description*—an evocation of what we eat. Naturally, there is no better place to turn to for that than a first-rate cookbook. Anyone who wants to know anything about American food can do no better than to run out and acquire a copy of Edna Lewis's magical and magisterial book, *The Taste of Country Cooking.* Miss Lewis, who in the opinion of many should be declared a living national treasure, was born in a rural Virginia town founded by freed slaves. As in most farming communities, food was taken seriously. People worked hard and ate well. Everything was made from scratch and there was no scrimping.

The Taste of Country Cooking is a memoir as well as a cookbook. It calls to mind a purer, more settled time in America, when the seasons were paramount and daily life revolved around them. In addition to the felicity of its prose, it offers numerous perfectly wonderful recipes. I can think of few things more inspiring than to curl up on a cold day with this book and a cup of coffee.

If a visitor came from Mars with questions about American food, I might steal into my daughter's room and purloin her copy of *Farmer Boy* by Laura Ingalls Wilder. Mrs. Wilder's Little

House books are filled with food, from slaughtering a pig to making a pie out of the blackbirds that destroyed Pa's corn crop. *Farmer Boy,* which is the story of Almanzo Wilder's childhood, relates that, at the County Fair, Almanzo "ate ham and chicken and turkey and dressing and cranberry jelly; he ate potatoes and gravy, succotash, baked beans and boiled beans and onions, and white bread and rye 'n' Injun bread and sweet pickles and jam and preserves. Then he drew a long breath and he ate pie." He eats pumpkin pie and custard pie and vinegar pie as well as mince pie. If these things intrigue your visitor, refer him or her to *The Little House Cookbook,* an excellent and beautiful volume by Barbara M. Walker, who tracked down the recipes for all the dishes mentioned in the Little House series—salt-rising bread, apple turnovers, stewed jackrabbit. It is clear from these books that part of American cooking (as it used to be) is a combination of thrift and lavishness: Every part of everything that could be used *was* used, and people ate lots and lots.

A more straightforward cookbook is Phillip Schulz's *As American as Apple Pie: 20 Best-Loved Dishes in 12 Sublime Variations.* The title is self-explanatory. Inside you will find twelve recipes each for such things as apple pie, chocolate cake, baked beans, fried chicken, stews, waffles, hash, and many more of our most beloved dishes. The recipes give an idea of regional variation as well as inspire the cook who is tired of his or her standard meat loaf or potato salad. Anyone who wants to cook like an American should have this book. Besides, twelve recipes for one dish is a plain old *luxury.*

I myself could not be without a copy of *Charleston Receipts,* first published in 1950 by the Junior League of Charleston and still going strong. It is a basic Southern cookbook, easy to use and delicious every time. It will help you make corn sticks, biscuits, and "short'nin' bread" (brown sugar shortbread, the kind "Mama's little baby loves") as well as oyster stew, hoppin' John (stewed black-eyed peas and rice, for which *As American as Apple Pie* has one of the best recipes I have ever tasted), and country captain (chicken stewed with tomato, curry, and raisins). My copy is splattered, dog-eared, and in constant use.

Naturally, no one, no matter how experienced in the kitchen, can manage without *Joy of Cooking* by Irma Rombauer. Mrs. Rombauer is to food what Dr. Spock is to babies. You can't run a kitchen or bring up an infant without them. The range of *Joy of Cooking* is amazing. It contains anything that anyone would ever want to cook, and there are people in this country who have never cooked from anything else.

My edition, which I acquired at a flea market, is from 1942. The *Joy*'s followers are like vintage wine–drinkers and have their favorite years. My copy was kind of falling apart when I bought it. Now it is held together by duct tape. Because it was published during the war, it has recipes for eggless cakes and long-lasting cookies that you could send to your boy overseas. The recipes are clear and will never fail you.

And now let us say it is a national holiday of some kind or another. You have invited guests from other countries (and perhaps other planets). What you want is a good old American meal that will reveal to your guests something of the nature of this country. You have assembled your cookbooks and now you must plan your meal.

For a first course, try something tangy: celery *rémoulade* from

New Orleans via France. This dish, for which there are endless recipes, requires celery root, peeled and cut into julienne strips and dressed hours in advance with mustard, mayonnaise, and lemon juice with a good spike of cayenne. On a bed of *arugula* it makes an admirable starter.

Next you must have fried chicken. It is a messy job, but you must do it for flag and country. Throw some old-time music on your player, find the recipe of your choice, and be prepared to stand over the stove for several hours. Your guests will adore you, and you will have been a good citizen.

Of course you must serve potato salad: There are dozens of recipes to choose from. Steamed corn if you are in the right season, succotash if not. You might also serve a big bowl of black beans and rice Cuban style, which is now about as American as anything else.

For dessert, the choices are endless: peach cobbler, apple crisp, brownies, bananas Foster. Or chocolate chip cookies made from the recipe on the chocolate morsels bag (you can't beat it). Or you can make my sister's peach pizza, a multicultural dessert that proves how ingenious we Americans are:

Leslie Friedman's Peach Pizza

1. Make a pastry by blending 1¼ cups flour, 1 teaspoon sugar, a pinch of salt, 1 stick ice-cold butter or margarine, and about 3 tablespoons ice water, or enough to form a dough. Form the dough into a disk, chill it, wrapped in plastic wrap, for ½ hour, and roll it out into a big circle or rectangle. Put the dough on a baking

sheet and turn up the edge to form a shallow rim. Chill the dough for 30 minutes.

2. Chop ½ cup almonds fine and add 2 tablespoons flour and 2 tablespoons sugar. Sprinkle the mixture over the dough.

3. Cut enough peeled peaches into thin slices to cover the dough in one layer in some attractive overlapping pattern and arrange them on the dough.

4. Bake the pizza at 375° F. for 30 minutes, or until the crust is golden.

If you peek under this meal you will find yourself in a number of other countries, immersed in other cuisines. As you look around your table—at which are seated, if you are lucky, congenial people from everywhere—you will realize the genius of American cooking and the secret of American life: a little bit of everything from everywhere put together to make something original and new.

Jet Lag and How to Feed It

Air travel is life's most democratic institution. It doesn't matter if you are a millionaire or a pauper, a wise man or a fool, the head of a multinational company or a student flying standby, at the end of your journey you will feel like hell. You may be returning from an invigorating trek through the Lake Country, or a tranquil week lying in the sun in Minorca, or a grueling week at the Frankfurt Book Fair, but by the time you get home you will be exhausted, dyspeptic, and confused, and you will also have a slight headache, aching sinuses, and cold feet.

Going away—that is, landing in a foreign place—is sufficiently exciting to make a person distracted. But flying to visit a friend is another matter. Staying with a friend, the jet-lagged person is like a newborn. He or she has survived the difficult passage of disembarking down that tiny aisle with a duffel plus carry-on baggage, the waiting for luggage, the agony of customs, and hailing a taxi, or waiting in the rain or snow for a bus. This wrecked person needs help, especially because it is eight at night in your cozy house and three in the morning in his brain. For a number of hours, as he flew through the air, time did not exist at all, since he was given lunch at what must have been midnight somewhere or other.

Airlines do not respect the biological clocks of most normal human beings. They do not land their airplanes at breakfast, lunch, or dinnertime, but whenever they feel like it. Thus the bedraggled traveler appears at eleven in the morning, three in the afternoon, or ten thirty at night, usually after having eaten something dreadful in a little plastic tray.

This person must be coddled, comforted, and made to know that something delicious but not taxing will be waiting for him to eat. The question is, What?

Recently I had a conversation with a friend who had just returned from an elaborate trip to Italy. She had been home for three hours, during which she had unpacked, taken a shower, and ordered a large, spicy Chinese meal to be sent in from the local Chinese restaurant. It takes all kinds, as they say (while I was waiting for my daughter to be born, all I could think about was a pastrami sandwich from the Carnegie Delicatessen), but on the whole, most people in situations of minor crisis would probably like a bowl of soup and an excellent sandwich.

There are certain things a jet-lagged person should *never* be given. Complicated pastry, such as a napoleon, should never even be shown to people who have been in an airport within the past ten hours. Nor should they be offered steak or grilled meat. An omelet sounds right but is in fact wrong. People in such tender condition must be given what is savory, and easy to digest—food that allows them to drift off gently into a much-needed nap.

After many years of experimenting, I have come up with what I believe to be the perfect meal for a jet-lagged person. Each part follows the other and gives reassurance. An orderly meal is restful.

The first course is lentil soup made with veal bones. The veal bones are essential. They give the soup a velvety, gelatinous quality that makes it slip easily into the stomach in an enriching manner. To this soup you may also add some pasta stars, or orzo. The combination of pasta and lentils, as we know, forms a perfect and digestible protein.

Next is a sandwich, which serves as a second course. A ham sandwich on white bread with parsley butter. If the person is a vegetarian, a cucumber sandwich and anchovy butter. The function of these sandwiches is to make the person drink the quantity of water he needs to replace because he has been dehydrated by the atmosphere of the cabin, which is like unto the Mojave desert. If you are a nice person you can serve half ham and half cucumber. A couple of tiny, spicy pickles are recommended as an aid to digestion.

The next course is a little plate of shortbread fingers (or shortbread cookies with a dot of raspberry jam). And finally, an orange. Or, if it is summer, a little plate of raspberries. After a meal like this, with lots of beer, the newly showered person can toddle off to dreamland while watching the evening news or pretending to read the morning paper.

The Egg and You

Once upon a time American citizens were told that eggs were bad for you and the eggs-and-bacon-for-breakfast-every-day boys were put on notice that their arteries were clogging and they had better lay off.

My family doctor, the late, great, and much-lamented Stephen B. Yohalem, a man who smoked his cigarettes unfiltered, thought this notion, like most, was a lot of hooey. He was for the golden mean and thought eating eggs every day was a dumb idea to begin with. His motto was, Never do anything for the sake of your health.

For years I meditated on this wisdom, as a kind of Jewish doctor's Zen koan, and I have come to think that what he meant is that we should be moderate, be sensible, and try to have a good time, too.

What this means in terms of eggs is this: If you are going to eat eggs, eat them once in a while, and make sure that you get your hands on really, really good ones.

There is no question about what constitutes a good egg. A good egg is one laid by a free-running chicken that eats organic feed and grubs around in the yard, unconfined to a battery hen-house in which debeaked, salmonella-ridden fowl are kept laying round the clock until they give out and are then made into cat food. And while some people think the whole idea of free-running birds is nonsense, let me be the first to tell them that how the hen lives makes a big difference to the egg.

An egg from a free-running chicken has a high, plump yolk. Unlike the pale, lemon yellow yolks we are used to from super-market eggs, these yolks are often brilliant orange. And they taste intensely like . . . like eggs: nutty, buttery, chickeny.

Once you have eaten an egg like this you will be reluctant to turn back, and nowadays it is easy not to. Many supermarkets sell organic eggs, and some even sell free-range eggs. They cost more, but if you are eating them once in a while, you can think of them as a kind of cheap luxury.

I am always on the lookout for wonderful eggs, and I espe-cially admire the green-shelled eggs laid by a variety of Peruvian chicken called the Ayacuna. These are sold at my local greenmar-ket by some women who run an herb farm and keep a small flock. In addition to the beauty of their shells, a pale, celadon green, they are about the most delicious eggs I have ever eaten. Many farms have small flocks and bring their eggs to the local farmers' market. But if you have no farmer's market, or your town has no health food store, go into your supermarket and nag the manager until he comes up with a source of organic eggs.

If you meet someone who keeps ducks, make that person into your very best friend at once. Duck eggs are ambrosial, and they are *big*, with dark orange yolks. Their shells are rather powdery, and they are much larger than even a jumbo egg. These taste like eggs to the tenth power and are definitely worth hunting for.

In my quest for eggs I have eaten pheasant eggs, which are smaller than small eggs and have a subtle, lovely taste; and quail eggs, which you can always buy in a Chinatown. These are tiny and speckled. You hard-cook them by slipping them into water that has just boiled and has been taken off the fire. Leave them for about seven minutes. They are hell to peel, and it is also sad to see those lovely speckled shells disintegrate. The quail egg is the gentle essence of egg. They are also perfect for a child's lunch box.

Now that you have acquired your eggs, what are you going to do with them?

In my opinion, the perfect form of egg is sunny side up, very gently cooked and covered until a pink, filmy veil forms over the yolk. These eggs should be served with very lightly buttered toast—this is an occasion, remember, not a daily event. Both eggs and toast get the merest sprinkle of salt and nothing else. You do not eat these for breakfast: You eat them for dinner when you are fully awake. Your taste buds have had a day to awaken, and you want a light meal.

Two of the greatest meals I have eaten in a long time were consumed during a recent summer, one in early June and one in August. Our local farm stand featured a sign that read "Last Asparagus." It was June and cold, and we were told that the asparagus was mostly gone, but we could buy what was left.

We tramped into the extensive asparagus patch, which was now mostly in fern. My daughter managed to spot a number of shoots. Children are good at this, being closer to the ground. These shoots were delicious, and we ate a number of them out of hand.

When we went to pay we found some fresh-picked spinach, and the farmer's wife offered us some eggs, which were new-laid. When we touched them they were *warm*.

Our dinner consisted of eggs over sautéed spinach and some lightly poached asparagus. Nothing was added to anything, except a little butter for the eggs. We had a nice loaf of bread and a little dish of salt, and all felt at home in the world for an hour or so, and reminded ourselves how good things taste when they are fresh.

The second great meal featured duck eggs. On the day that a friend gave me half a dozen, we had a howling storm that took down some large trees and left our driveway festooned with electrical lines. Within a half hour we were host to the fire squad and a party of workers from Power and Light. We were also starving, and our electric stove was dead as a dinosaur.

We filled two baskets with produce and set off through the woods—our road was blocked by live wires and tree trunks—to our neighbor's house, where, with the aid of candles, we cooked fried potatoes and duck eggs on his gas stove. A dinner of home fries, steamed corn, and one duck egg apiece is a very good thing, especially when, after it, you find that the road is clear, the moon is out, and bright lights are back on again at your house.

Four Easy Pieces

Every working woman dreams about two things: more time and a cook. If you have a family, someone must feed it, and if you do not happen to have a cook and you happen to be a woman, most likely the person doing the cooking will be you, and you will be doing it at the last minute in a frazzled state after a long day at the office.

Since I work at home, everyone assumes I have absolutely nothing whatsoever to do all day except shop and cook. When two or three working mothers are gathered together, the subject of cooking invariably comes up, but I am thought to be exempt from this conversation because my office is my bedroom and I do not commute to it by bus.

There is no question about it: Being home does give a person more time, but in my case not much more. Work must get done and dinner must still be produced. There are of course ways around this: cans, things you heat up in microwavable packages, and takeout. I know a woman whose three-year-old son thought that *Chinese food* was the generic term for "meal" and when given his cereal for breakfast or cheese sandwich for lunch would cry out happily: "Chinese food! Chinese food!"

But consider the case of a friend I will call Pat S. (not her real name). She has a full-time job, a husband, and a six-year-old daughter. To complicate her culinary life, she lives in one of those not yet gentrified parts of town in which the only supermarket is a ten-block walk: There is not so much as a bodega or candy store nearby. On her way home from work she could easily buy a new transistor radio, a discount sweater, or a My First Sony tape recorder, but she would be hard put to buy a piece of bubble gum let alone a quart of milk. And so her shopping gets done on Saturday morning, a day on which a working mother might like to have five or six minutes of spare time. This shopping sweepstakes plunges her into a depressing frenzy of menu planning, and there is no margin for error. Not for her the string bag full of delicious last-minute purchases from a lovely shop around the corner. Around the corner is a parking lot, a carpet warehouse, and a discount appliance shop.

Despite these unhelpful circumstances, Pat S. comes home at night and sets about preparing what I would call a real midwestern meal, with representatives from all the correct food groups plus dessert. When I first met her and she revealed this to me, I assumed that anyone compelled to produce veal stew with green olives, mashed potatoes, ham with Madeira and cream sauce, buttered noodles, pepper steak, and meat loaf on a daily basis must be a nut. But now that I have come to know her, I think she is heroic. She wants her family to sit down to a real meal with real food, and she is not alone.

I have come to the conclusion that the working woman's best friend is a flame tamer. This innocent gizmo, which can be purchased in any hardware store, is actually a flame disperser. People who are pressed for time will discover that they can put a pot of soup or stew on a flame tamer over a low flame and *leave their house*. You can imagine how liberating this can be.

During my years of working motherhood I have come up with some good old reliable standbys, all of which have been extensively child tested. My requirements for a reliable standby is that it be delicious, be easy to make, and (with one exception) be able to be prepared while I am doing something else. I like old-fashioned food, so these standbys are decidedly not trendy.

The first of these is soup—good for dinner, good for lunch, and a hit when put in a thermos and into the lunch box. Scotch broth is a soup almost no one makes from scratch anymore (although it is readily available in cans). It is extremely easy to make and good for you. You can make it on the weekend and keep it in the fridge, or you can put it together before you go to sleep and let it simmer the night away on the flame tamer. I make it in two easy stages, but it can probably be made in one.

For four people you need 1 meaty lamb shank, a cheap cut of meat usually available in even a nasty supermarket, 2 (or more) big cloves of garlic, 1 unpeeled onion (the skin gives the broth a nice color), about 8 cups of water, and a low flame. Put a cover on the pot, the flame tamer underneath it, and go about your business. Hours later strain the soup, cut up the meat, put it in a jar or bowl, and let it sit in the fridge. When you are ready, skim off the fat, put the broth and meat in a pot, and 1½ cups of barley and 1 sliced carrot and let simmer for half an hour. A tablespoon of tomato paste is nice. Salt to taste. If you hate lamb, substitute one small chicken with skin and fat removed and you will have made chicken and barley soup. This soup is good for invalids, and for children recovering from colds and gastrointestinal disorders.

If you happen to be a vegetarian, or run with vegetarians, or don't eat very much meat, vegetarian chili is calling out to you. This recipe, which is embarrassingly simple and always tastes wonderful, has also been intensively child tested, even on picky eaters. You need 1 cup black beans; 1 cup little red beans; 1 chopped onion; 2 big cloves of garlic, minced; and a large can of plum tomatoes, juice and all, plus 2 to 3 cups of water. These ingredients go into a pot, the pot goes on top of the flame tamer, and you go out. In four hours you have vegetarian chili, which the next day can be heated up and put into someone's lunch box.

If I had a dollar for every time someone said to me, "I don't have time to bake bread anymore," I would be as rich as Donald Trump used to be. If you tell people you bake your own bread they look at you with either contempt or disbelief. If you tell them it's a snap, they say cheerlessly, "A snap for *you*." But it *is* a snap, and I have done it. This recipe produces two loaves, one for sandwiches, and one for the world's best toast.

1. An hour before you go to bed, fling 1 cup oatmeal into your blender and grind. Put the oatmeal, 1 cup of wheat germ, 6 cups of white flour, 1 tablespoon of salt, and ½ teaspoon of yeast into a large bowl. About 3 cups of tepid water will make up the dough. Knead it, roll it in

flour, and put it right back in the bowl you mixed it up in. Cover the bowl and go to sleep.

2. The next morning, make the coffee and knock down the bread. Divide it in half and put each half into a buttered bread tin (you can butter them the night before and stick them in the fridge to save time). Cover the tins with a tea towel and go to work.

3. When you come home, heat the oven to 400° F., paint the top of the loaves with milk (this is a frill and need not be done, but it makes a nice-looking crust), and bake for about 40 minutes, turning once. It is hard to describe the nutty, buttery taste of this bread, and it is worth the 15 minutes of work it took you to make.

Now that you have had your soup and chili and bread, it is time to think about dessert. Dessert is, in my opinion, totally unnecessary as part of a meal, and we would all be better off if we finished our dinner with an apple, but every now and again, everyone wants a piece of homemade cake, and naturally, no one thinks there is any time to make it.

Recently I became addicted to the kind of classic, basic sponge cake English women of a certain age can make in their sleep. It is generally used as a plain tea cake, spread with raspberry jelly and dusted with powdered sugar. It is absolutely delicious, and, best of all, it has four ingredients. If you want to be snooty you can call it a *génoise*. I use a 7-inch round tin, but an 8-inch square is fine.

Cream 1 stick of sweet butter and ½ cup of sugar. Beat in

2 eggs (or 1 yolk and 2 whites). Beat until light and fluffy with either a whisk or an electric beater. Fold in 1 cup of flour to which you have added ½ teaspoon baking powder and 1 teaspoon of vanilla, if you like. (You can do without the baking powder or the vanilla.) Bake in a buttered tin for 20 minutes to half an hour. You can eat this cake plain, with stewed fruit, or with ice cream, but it is best with jam and powdered sugar. For grown-ups, bitter marmalade is *very* nice. Your actual work time is about ten minutes, which produces one of the best cakes you will ever eat.

These easy recipes give back a thousand times what you put into them. For the harried mother, they are a lifesaver. They do not involve nasty shortcuts—shortcuts are quite unnecessary. I love the idea of something waiting on the stove when I come home, and I find myself grateful for things that simply cook themselves.

It goes without saying that if you can provision organic ingredients, everything will taste better (and you will sleep better knowing that your loved ones are not stuffed with pesticides and chemical residues). Most health food stores have organic flour (even white flour), and a trip to the greenmarket is worth it for organic eggs, free-range chickens, and hormone-free meat. Many people resent the idea of large corporations dictating what their children eat. These easy dishes give you some control over what your family is ingesting.

Our present lives, in which two people have to work like dogs simply to keep up, are hard on everybody. In our hearts we long for someone to help us out. User-friendly recipes—a score of soups and stews and breads of infinite variety—do help us out.

No matter how hard we work, we must also eat. To sit down

with family and friends to a good meal is nourishing not only to the body but to the spirit. If our world is heartless, we must start somewhere. A bowl of soup and a piece of good bread provide a haven and help us get back that sense of a family dinner and a homemade meal.

American Corn

It is hard to believe, but sometime around August people actually get sick of eating corn on the cob. Your family and friends who once greeted the sight of you bearing an immense platter of freshly steamed ears now look up from their places and say in one despondent voice, "Corn? Again?"

This usually happens a few hours after you have hit your local farm stand and bought enough to feed four ears to everyone. Worse still, you may already have cooked it, and now you are stuck.

The obvious answer to this horrible problem is to serve corn off the cob. Failing that, a new family or new friends are definitely in order.

Your first problem is to get the corn *off* the cob. Anyone with any experience in this line will tell you that there is nothing for flying around a kitchen like a corn kernel. Most people face this with a sharp knife and a deep bowl, but others are more ingenious.

My friend Janice Bracken in West Cornwall, Connecticut, has tackled this problem with fiendish cleverness. A trauma nurse and art printer, she is not about to be stymied by an ear of corn.

To get her corn off the cob she invested in a devilish French gizmo that features a flexible metal ring embedded in a sheet of plastic. You fit the ring over the corn, pull down, and *voilà!* On the first try the ear of corn slipped under the pressure of the ring and corn kernels got all over the floor.

And so, in the American spirit of ingenuity, Mrs. Bracken went the French device one better. She pounded two nails, sharp side up, into a board that fit over her sink. She impaled the ear of corn on the nails, slipped on the French gizmo, and watched with pride as the entire ear was dekerneled into a waiting dish in the sink.

I myself am still in the sharp knife/deep bowl stage, but whatever is your method you will soon end up with a large bowl of naked corn kernels, and the question is, what to do with them.

You can put some into your pancake batter or throw some into your corn bread. You can make a lovely corn salad, with cooked or uncooked corn, chopped roasted red peppers, string beans, and plenty of dressing heavy on garlic and lemon juice. You can put some into your vegetable soup or make corn chowder out of it.

If you are having unexpected company, you can impress your guests with a salad of corn, red peppers, black beans, and avocado to which you might add crabmeat (if you live near the ocean or have come into an inheritance) or cold leftover chicken or some sautéed shrimp. On a bed of greens this makes a beautiful lunch, and with the addition of a nice goat cheese and a loaf of bread you needn't serve another thing.

One of the easiest and most savory things you can do with corn off the cob comes from *Ismail Merchant's Indian Cuisine.*

Mr. Merchant is a film producer and a man around the kitchen. Although not long on text, this is a very personal book that demonstrates how one person fused the traditions of his homeland with that of his adopted homeland. His recipe must be made with fresh corn, and it is worth waiting a whole year to get it.

Cut as much fresh, uncooked corn as you have people to feed. Sauté it gently in butter. Add a pinch of salt and cayenne pepper to taste. It can be as mild or hot as you like. Cook a few minutes and then add a splash of cream (half-and-half or even milk will do). Cook a little more and serve hot. This multicultural dish is mellow and sweet as well as spicy and suave. With a side dish of *basmati* rice it is pure heaven.

If you are feeding friends from other countries, corn fritters are what you are looking for. Since they are no longer fashionable you can even find red-blooded Americans who haven't eaten them since childhood.

For four people you need about 6 ears of corn. The batter is made with 4 ounces of flour, 4 tablespoons of olive oil, a pinch of salt into the yolk, and a pint of warm water, plus 1 egg, separated, and the white beaten until stiff.

Stir the oil and water into the flour slowly, and add the beaten yolk. Then fold in the stiffly beaten white of egg. Let sit for an hour. Before frying, add the corn.

You can fry these fritters in anything you like. I prefer olive oil with a smashed clove of garlic, but light sesame oil would be very good, too. Fry until golden on both sides (or brown if you like them crisper), drain on paper towels, and try not to eat them all standing up in the kitchen.

Some people like these with applesauce, as in potato pancakes. Some like them with maple syrup. But I like mine with *salsa* on the side.

This is a summer dish, and *salsa* can only be made in the summer. You need some big, ripe tomatoes, 1 brand-new onion, 1 sweet green pepper, and a pepper as hot as you can stand. Dice everything up and dress with olive oil, celery salt, lime juice, and some minced garlic. Children probably won't like this, but grownups do.

One bite of these fritters and you will have your friends telling you about their days at summer camp when they lined up at the kitchen hatchway begging the cook for a few more.

That is the magic of corn, America's most emblematic food. It evokes memories of sunburn and rowing and swimming in the lake or wandering on the beach looking for shells. It is true soul food and requires of the exhausted cook nothing more than a large pot of boiling water and some people willing to do the shucking. Furthermore, it provides entertainment for small children, who find corn silk irresistible.

Now that you have made your corn bread and your corn salad, the fritters and Ismail Merchant's spiced corn and you still have corn left over, fate has called out to you that you must make corn relish. I did not resist this call. I made corn relish from Helen Witty's irreplaceable, invaluable, and all-around excellent book *Fancy Pantry*. As a result (I am not ashamed to reveal) my corn relish won a blue ribbon at the agricultural fair in Cornwall, Connecticut. The tasters were Alice Cadwell, who with her husband, David, owns Cadwell's Corner, a breakfast and luncheon institution, and Sue Kochman, the proprietor of the New England Catering Company in Cornwall Bridge. Getting a blue ribbon from them made me feel that I had won the Nobel Prize.

Blue-Ribbon Corn Relish
(adapted from Fancy Pantry by Helen Witty)

Combine in a large pan or preserving pan: 6 cups uncooked corn; 1 large red pepper, diced; 1 green pepper, diced; about 1 to 1½ cups dark brown sugar (depending on how sweet you like it); 2 tablespoons kosher salt; 2 tablespoons dry mustard; 1½ teaspoons ground celery seed (or use celery salt and cut the amount of salt), ¼ teaspoon cayenne pepper (or use hot peppers to taste—I like this *really* hot); and 1¼ cups of cider vinegar. At the last moment you will add 2 cups diced onions.

Remember that corn relish, like chutney, is friendly and hard to mess up. If you have no mustard, use something else: turmeric, *garam masala,* curry powder. Taste is the deciding factor. Bring all this, except for the onions, to a boil, then lower to a simmer. When the mixture begins to cook down, which takes about 15 to 20 minutes, add the onions. If you put them in at the last minute, they stay crunchy. Ladle into sterilized jars, seal with two-piece lids, and stick the jars in a boiling water bath up to their necks for about 15 minutes.

You will never have to buy Christmas presents again. Your friends will be delighted (or initially puzzled but ultimately delighted) by this. Many people have never had corn relish, and it is up to you to educate them.

And even when everyone is sick of corn on the cob, you never have to pass a "Fresh Corn" sign without stopping for an armload or two.

Jam Anxiety

It took me a long time to get over my fear of making jam. The whole enterprise seemed terrifying. After all, entire *factories* were devoted to its manufacture, so how was I, one small person in an inadequate kitchen, supposed to compete?

Besides, I am not much of a jam eater, but I am married to a man of European descent. He was born in Latvia and came to this country when he was seven, so he is totally Americanized. But the first time I saw him tuck into a plate of pancakes topped with jam, I realized he was a foreigner after all. Europeans do not eat maple syrup on their pancakes, possibly because the sugar maple is indigenous to North America.

In short, jam is a staple of our household, and it is not uncommon for me to crawl out of bed on Saturday or Sunday (Ma's morning off) to find my husband and our half-Latvian daughter happily eating pancakes (more like crêpes) rolled up with jam inside.

There is nothing more daunting than to visit someone's country house and see a jelly cupboard actually filled with homemade jam and jelly, neatly labeled, row upon row. I once visited a classic supermom on an island in Maine: no running water, no electricity. One wood stove and an outhouse. Above her stove was rigged a massive jelly bag, which dripped into a kettle. She and her children had collected wild apples, and she was making jelly out of them. *I am a worm,* I thought to myself.

Not being much of a jam eater, I did not think much about the contents of these gleaming jars until last year, when a friend of mine gave me a spoonful of her homemade raspberry jam. Now you can spend a fortune on jam. You can go to tiny shops in Paris that put their jams up in beautiful little pots, but there is nothing like good homemade jam. It is hard to pin down exactly what is so wonderful about it, but it is *wonderful.* It tastes cleaner, clearer, more . . . immediate. The fruit tastes bright and forthright, the sugar somewhat recessive. *This is definitely worth looking into,* I thought.

Then my mother-in-law appeared with a jar of plum jelly made by a friend of hers whose name, unless you have had extensive contact with Latvians, is unpronounceable. It was, hands down, the most delicious jelly I have ever tasted: deep, intense, not too sweet, with a beautiful silky consistency and a clean, profound taste of plums. Then and there I decided I would make jam. But what jam to make?

I felt I ought to take it easy and make something out of a fruit high in pectin, since the idea of pouring commercial pectin into fruit somehow makes my flesh creep. I wanted to make jam I couldn't buy (or couldn't buy easily), and I was sorry I had not had this marvelous idea when the greengage plums were in season, since I do love greengage jam.

Plum was what I decided upon anyway, since plum jam seems to be a specialty item. Once I made my decision, anxiety set in, and I realized that of course I had no idea how to make jam. And so I began first to read and then to nag my jam-making friends who said not to worry—jam making was a snap, they said.

As usual, reading other people's recipes confused me utterly. The words *candy thermometer* depressed me—I have no such implement in my house. Also, I am notoriously hopeless at math and once was put in the humiliating position of having to call one of my writing students on the telephone (this young woman is of course exceedingly brilliant) and ask her how many cups of flour I would need to double a three-and-three-quarters-cup recipe.

The ratio I decided on was four pounds of fruit to three pounds of sugar. Like a good girl I went out and bought a nice, cheap, well-designed kitchen scale. I bought those big purple prune plums, and since no recipe said anything about taking the skin off or leaving it on, I decided to cut the fruit up fine and leave the skin on for the color. Alas, I had three pounds of fruit. "That means two pounds of sugar, right?" I said to my husband, who is also pretty decrepit at math. "No," he said. "It doesn't."

"Well, what then?" I asked.

"I can't find my calculator," he said.

"That's all right," I said. "Let's call Audrey."

Audrey Jacobson is my oldest friend. She is a doctor and is at present the director of health for the Board of Education. You would think she might be left in peace but no, I dialed her at once.

"If I have three pounds of fruit, how much sugar do I need if the original recipe calls for four pounds of fruit to three pounds of sugar?"

"Two and a quarter," she said immediately. I was speechless at her genius.

"How did you figure that out?" I gasped.

"It's simple, dear," said Audrey, who in medical school used to read Jorge Luis Borges for relaxation and at college did calculus problems to calm down. What she explained cannot be reproduced by me since it went in one head, as they say, and out the other.

I followed the recipe, which called for a pint of water, but I forgot to increase the amount. I also used white and turbinado sugar since that's what I had lying around. It took a long time for this mixture to do whatever it was supposed to do. The recipes tell you to put little spoonfuls of the cooking jam into a dish and see if it holds its shape or drop it into water and see if it forms a ball, or stick a thermometer in it to see what its temperature is.

What they don't tell you is that when it has turned into jam, it *looks* like jam. It is thick and has the consistency of cold molasses. At this point you take your tongs, get the canning jars out of their boiling water bath, and pad them up. These days you do not need to drip flammable paraffin on top: The jars seal themselves.

Once my jars were labeled, I felt contenedly thrilled with myself, as if I had pulled off a wonderful trick. People feel this way when they bake bread or have babies, and although they are perfectly entitled to feel that way, in fact, nature does most of the work. Jam making *is*, actually, a snap, and also very liberating, since once you know how, you realize it is not the project of an entire day or week (jelly making is quite another matter) but half an evening's pleasant and rewarding effort. And, of course, jam is a wonderful thing to give away, if you can bear to part with it.

Plum Jam

1. Buy 4 pounds of prune plums and wash them well. It is preferable to use plums that have never been sprayed, if you can find them. This will fill six 8-ounce jars with some left over to put into a clean mayonnaise jar for instant consumption.

2. Cut them into thin slices and weigh them. Without the stones, 4 pounds of plums gives about 3 pounds of fruit. If you don't have a scale, the rule seems to be 1 cup of fruit to a scant ¾ cup of sugar.

3. Put the plums in a heavy, enameled cast-iron pot along with about a cup of filtered water. Gradually add the sugar—I would use 2 pounds and forget about the exact mathematical ratios (and eventually I will see if I can make it even less sweet)—and begin to boil.

4. Sit down with a good book and a wooden spoon and let the plums boil gently. Stir them from time to time, rather more frequently than not. The juice of half a lime or lemon should be squeezed in at one point.

5. While the jam is cooking, boil the jars and lids, write out your labels, and when the plums are the color of Passover wine and are thick and jamlike, take them off the fire and spoon the jam into the jars. Cover and seal.

The next morning open one of your jars. There, to your utter amazement, will be delicious plum jam, made by you with *your* name on the label. Now you are in a position to make someone who does not make jam feel like a worm, or you can be a pal and explain that it takes, really and truly, almost no time at all.

Three Chocolate Cakes

Anyone who spends any time in the kitchen eventually comes to realize that what she or he is looking for is the perfect chocolate cake. My sister, whose lifelong addiction to chocolate is almost like a religion (including bouts of fasting followed by celebration), feels she has the perfect recipe, one that calls for a whole can of chocolate syrup. Snootier types turn up their noses at the very idea, though, and I myself tend toward melted chocolate squares and unsweetened cocoa powder.

For a few years my chocolate cake of choice was one found in Elizabeth David's *French Provincial Cooking,* the volume of which I own a paperback with a rubber band around its middle to keep the pages from falling out. It is especially damaged on the page for *gâteau au chocolat et aux amandes,* a flourless chocolate cake made with ground almonds that tastes like a transcendent form of fudge and is a wonderful thing to serve at Passover.

This cake is made in a springform pan, the bottom of which serves as its plate. To make it takes a little bit of time, but it is time well spent. People simply moan at the taste: It is perhaps the king and queen of all chocolate cakes.

Elizabeth David's Flourless Chocolate Cake

1. Preheat the oven to 300° F. and butter an 8-inch spring-form pan.

2. In a heavy saucepan over low heat melt 4 ounces bit-tersweet (not unsweetened) chocolate with 1 teaspoon vanilla and 1 tablespoon each brewed espresso (or any very strong coffee) and brandy.

3. Add 6 tablespoons butter, ½ cup sugar, and ½ cup ground almonds (I never bother to blanch the almonds but stick them in the blender skin and all) and heat the mixture until the butter is melted. Remove the pan from the heat.

4. Beat 3 large egg yolks until they are lemon colored and stir them into the chocolate mixture.

5. Whip 3 large egg whites until they are just stiff and fold them into the chocolate mixture.

6. Turn the batter into the pan and bake the cake in the middle of the oven for 45 minutes. The cake will have some cracks on top and a tester will not come out clean. Let the cake cool completely on a rack and remove the side of the pan.

The cake will rise and then fall. It can be brushed with raspberry jelly or covered with whipped cream. More leisured types can put the jelly or whipped cream in a pastry bag fitted with a fancy tip and draw designs with it or form the whipped cream into leaves or swags. Lazier people get away with a blob of whipped cream or *crème fraîche* on the side, and minimalists will find that a plain scattering of powdered sugar is nice enough.

This cake is also excellent with vanilla ice cream if you want to go whole hog.

You never know where you will find a recipe. They are often hidden in unexpected places. I did not anticipate finding a chocolate cake in a children's book, but in a small, charming volume titled *Happy Winter,* written and illustrated by Karen Gundersheimer, I did. This book, which was one of my daughter's early favorites, tells a story in rhyme about two sisters on a snowy day. When they have finished playing dress-up and going outside to make snow angels, they come indoors to help their mother make a fudge cake. The recipe is given in rhyme and then written out on the facing page. It is easy, wholesome, and delicious and has now become my daughter's standard birthday cake.

Happy Winter Fudge Cake

1. Preheat the oven to 350° F. and butter a 9½- by 3-inch springform pan fitted with the tube bottom.
2. Melt 3 squares semisweet chocolate in a heavy saucepan over low heat and let the chocolate cool.
3. In a bowl mix 2 cups flour, 1 cup sugar, 1 tablespoon cocoa powder, and 1 teaspoon each baking powder and baking soda.
4. In another bowl with a mixer mix 2 eggs, 4 tablespoons softened butter, cut in little pieces, 1 teaspoon vanilla, and 1½ cups plain yogurt and then beat in the melted chocolate.

5. Add the wet ingredients to the dry ones and add 1 cup chocolate morsels, large or small.

6. Turn the batter into the pan and bake the cake in the middle of the oven for 45 minutes. The cake will pull away slightly from the side of the pan. Let the cake cool for 30 minutes, remove the side of the pan, and invert the cake onto a plate, removing the bottom of the pan.

I make this cake in a springform tube pan with a scalloped bottom, and so it has a lovely scalloped top when it is turned out. If you own one of those fancy cake-decorating kits that come with a pastry nail and dozens of tubes you will never use because you can't figure out what they do, for this occasion you might produce some passable-looking roses and scatter them among the scallops, connecting them with green leaves. (Leaves are *easy* compared to roses.) The result is eccentric looking in a sort of demented Victorian way, but this cake is a hit with children who do not mind an uniced cake if it has *tons* of sugar roses. (A good rule for any birthday party is: a rose for every child.)

One afternoon when our daughters were on an outing with their fathers, my friend Karen Edwards, a former *sous-chef* at the old Tenth Avenue Bar in New York City, and I were sitting around in terrible moods caused by exhaustion and low blood sugar. Then she presented me with a slice of a delicious chocolate cake. Because Karen is not in the habit of baking chocolate cakes, I asked her why she had done so. It turns out that like everyone else she is searching for the one true chocolate cake, and it is her further requirement that it be extremely easy.

This cake comes from the new *Fanny Farmer Cookbook*, revised by Marion Cunningham, and whoever thought the recipe up ought to get the Nobel Prize. It is awesomely simple, contains no eggs, can be made in one bowl, and calls for only ½ cup of vegetable oil (cheaters can use melted butter). The original recipe has been tinkered with to good effect.

Karen Edwards's Version of Buttermilk Cocoa Cake

1. Preheat the oven to 350° F. and butter and flour a 9- by 2-inch round cake pan.
2. Mix together 1¾ cups flour, ¾ cup unsweetened cocoa powder, 1 cup sugar, 1 teaspoon baking soda, and ¼ teaspoon salt.
3. To these ingredients add 1 cup buttermilk, ½ cup vegetable oil or melted butter, and 2 teaspoons vanilla. Mix.
4. Turn the batter into the pan, bake the cake in the middle of the oven for 30 minutes, or until a tester comes out clean, and let it cool for 5 minutes before turning it out of the pan.

It is hard to encapsulate the virtues of this cake. It is fast, easy, and scrumptious. It has a velvety, powdery feel—the result of all that cocoa. It is not so horribly bad for you, because you use buttermilk, which is relatively low in fat, and cocoa powder is defatted anyway. Furthermore, it keeps like a dream and tastes even better after a few days.

If you want to be lavish you can dress this cake up by serving it with ice cream or *crème fraîche*. This mitigates its purist, min-imalist virtues, but that is the way of chocolate cakes. They are good in themselves but sometimes call out for window dressing. You can eat them gussied up with all sorts of rich and fattening things or you can leave them quite alone and serve them in pris-tine, solitary splendor on a nice white plate.

And while you savor them, you can keep in mind that there are *hundreds* more out there.

In Praise of Pears

In the world of fruit, pears are a cook's greatest ally. Imagine, a fruit that ripens off the tree: Bought hard as a rock and kept on the counter, it becomes juicy, smooth, and perfect in just a few days. Like the quince, the pear perfumes a room. Unlike the quince, which is tricky to cook, the pear cooks like a dream. You can poach pears in wine or syrup or bake them like apples. They may be turned into a heavenly cake or peeled and sliced and served with walnuts and blue cheese. You can compose a salad around sliced pears with some *frisée,* a little arugula for snap, and a spicy dressing to which you might want to add a dash of curry.

For my money you can't beat a Bartlett pear or its close relative the Clapp's Favorite. I like an Anjou or a Comice, too, but neither is ever as slurpy, never says "pear," like the Bartlett. And the Bosc doesn't either, though it is still the best pear for baking or poaching because it holds its shape and does not get mushy.

I first made poached pears in the kitchen of the man who would later become my husband. He had bought a nice bottle of Beaujolais Nouveau, and I thought I would use some of it to poach the fruit. As the pears were simmering, I decided to take a little nip. *My*, I thought, *this is* fizzy. It tasted like a kind of sublime grape pop but not as sweet. By the time the pears were ready, the rest of the wine had been consumed without so much as a drop left for my sweetheart, but I was quite cheerful.

Since then, I have poached pears in other red wines, white wine, cider, and water and sugar—often with cinnamon or lemon peel or cloves. They are practically idiot-proof and are loved by even the tiniest children. Poached pears can be put in a Happy Baby food grinder and given to your tot. These taste much better than the puréed pears that come out of a baby-food jar, though the store-bought product is, in my opinion, pretty good.

For the lazy, the exhausted, and the overtaxed, the best dessert is a ripe pear served on a plate with a small knife. One of those dangerous *triple-crème* cheese—Explorateur, Boursault, or St. André—would go with it magnificently. This is all you need to serve even the swankiest guest. For a few weeks in the fall, I find red pears at my market. Juicy as Bartletts but much more decorative, they look lavishing and extravagant on a white dish—always a fitting touch at the end of a party.

For the slightly more ambitious, I recommend a really easy pear dessert from an English book entitled *Josceline Dimbleby's Book of Puddings, Desserts and Savouries*, a treasured text now falling apart. Anyone who has British friends would do well to have one of them send this book over. The recipes are uncomplicated and delicious.

This one is for Chocolate Pear Pudding. You peel, core, and slice thin (or cut into chunks) 1 pound of pears, which you arrange on the bottom of a buttered baking dish, sprinkle with sugar, and dot with about 2 tablespoons butter. You then mix together ¾ cup flour, 1 generous tablespoon unsweetened cocoa powder, ½ teaspoon baking soda, ½ teaspoon baking powder, a scant ¾ cup dark brown sugar, 2 tablespoons Lyle's Golden Syrup (now generally available), 1 large egg, beaten, 4 tablespoons melted butter, and ¼ cup milk and beat it all into a batter. The whole performance takes about 20 minutes. Pour the batter on top of the pears and bake the pudding for 45 to 50 minutes in a 325° F. oven. This pudding can be eaten hot, cold, or at room temperature and is especially good with ice cream.

In my neighborhood there is a New Age Mexican restaurant called the Bright Food Shop. It serves chili and corn bread and *posole* as well as a number of wonderful made-up things. For dessert the restaurant once served a Lemon Pear Crisp that I felt instantly compelled to replicate in my own home. It is a total breeze: Slice or chunk around 4 pounds of pears as you would for apple crisp, toss them in ¼ cup lemon juice and sugar to taste (I use just a little, but you could add up to ¼ cup), and place them in a large baking pan. If you want to be fancy, put a sprig of rosemary in the bottom, although I would omit it if children are among your guests. Then rub together ¾ cup brown sugar, 1 cup flour, and 1 stick butter, grate in the yellow skin of a lemon, and sprinkle the topping over the pears. Bake the crisp for 30 to 35 minutes in a 400° F. oven. The result is satisfying and altogether a hit.

If you happen to have a pear tree or have come into more pears than you know what to do with, pear chutney is your solution. Even people who never thought of putting up anything at all, or who just once made a few jars of strawberry jam, might be lured by pear chutney. It makes a great holiday gift. You can stir it while on the phone with a friend, and you don't have to worry about setting points.

Pear Chutney is friendly and foolproof. Sterilize eight 8-ounce jars, though you may not need all eight. Cook together 3 pounds firm-ripe pears, cored (but not peeled) and chopped, 2 big cloves of garlic, minced, 2 teaspoons salt, 2 teaspoons hot paprika (or cayenne to taste), 2 teaspoons ground coriander (use whole coriander seeds and crush them yourself), 1 cup vinegar or lime juice or a combination of both, 1½ cups raisins (in a pinch I have used chopped prunes, with great success), and 2 tablespoons minced fresh ginger (or 1 tablespoon ground dried). When the pears are tender, stir in 1 cup brown sugar. If the chutney seems too thick, add about ½ cup water. Then cook it down for around 10 minutes—until it is sludgy but not liquidy. Put it in the sterilized jars, seal the jars, and process them for 10 minutes. Keep the jars for a few months before opening.

After you have made this chutney and have discovered how easy it is, you will gain confidence and courage and can start fooling around with the recipe to suit yourself, adding onion or allspice—whatever. I have used garlic vinegar, preserved ginger, currants. The original version of this recipe, from *The Penguin Book of Jams, Pickles and Chutneys*, by David and Rose Mabey (an English couple who write about food), calls for celery, which I usually leave out but could certainly be put back in. This chutney, like so many chutneys, is flexible. Of course it is nicest to cook it while drinking a glass of Beaujolais Nouveau and eating a really fine ripe pear.

Roast Chicken

There is nothing like roast chicken. It is helpful and agreeable, the perfect dish no matter what the circumstances. Elegant or homey, a dish for a dinner party or a family supper, it will not let you down.

In the fall it is uplifting served with celery *rémoulade,* and it is comforting in the winter with bread and mushroom stuffing. Or it is just the thing for a spring dinner stuffed with green grapes or half a lemon. In the summer it is nice to roast your chicken in the morning, let it cool off in the fridge, and serve it cold for dinner. This jells the juices and brings out the chicken flavor. Cold roast chicken, with or without garlic mayonnaise, is my idea of pure heaven.

The best chickens are free-range, organic birds. This means that they have been left to run around and scratch in the barnyard and have not been packed like rush-hour commuters in henhouses to be factory-farmed. If you can find them, get them. They turn up at farmers' markets, at health food stores, and now and again at fancy butchers'. In my opinion, the cooks of this country ought to begin a nagging campaign until butchers everywhere make them available. They cost more and they taste better. Everything else simply makes do, but some roast chicken is in the end better than no roast chicken.

As you approach your bird you will realize that there is controversy on the subject of roasting time. Some people think that chicken should be ever so slightly underdone, pink at the joints. Fifteen minutes a pound tops is their advice.

I, on the other hand, like my chicken roasted until the meat falls off the bone and the skin is very crisp. If you tell people that you roast a three-pound chicken for almost three hours they gasp with horror. "But it must be completely dry!" they shriek.

Actually, it is completely moist and juicy, crisp and tender, all at the same time. The secret is to slow-roast at between 250° and 300° F. and baste constantly. This is the chicken of my childhood, and it is the chicken you get at my mother's and sister's houses, and none of us has ever had any protests.

The simplest chicken is stuffed with a couple of cloves of garlic and half a lemon. My mother seasons the skin with paprika, salt, and pepper, and so do I. The paprika gives the skin a deep, lovely color, a nice crunch, and the merest hint of smokiness.

A few green grapes in the cavity of the chicken make an elegant dish. You spill them out into the pan juices, which, when spiked with a drop or two of lemon juice, make a delicious sauce.

More down home, but just the thing after a long day, is chicken roasted with vegetables. It is easy, too. A couple of peeled, sliced potatoes, carrots, and onions are sautéed in butter and then tipped into the roasting pan. You can season them with thyme or rosemary and pepper. You set the seasoned chicken in their midst like an ocean liner amongst tugs, and the result gives you a main course and vegetables.

If you happen to have some good whole-wheat bread around, dice it up with some chopped fungi *porcini,* toss in butter, and add broth to moisten for a stuffing that is both down-home and upscale at the same time.

A chicken roasted with little white onions and tiny new potatoes makes an appealing dish. You can mash up the potatoes on your plate and pour the pan juice on top. This is often a hit with young children, who, if they don't like white potatoes, are often mad for onions. They can put the whole onion in their mouth or smack it with a fork and watch what looks like a procession of little onions emerge.

Those who eschew fat but still want some roast chicken in their lives can satisfy themselves by removing the crisp skin and giving it to a deserving friend with low cholesterol and pouring all the pan juices and the juice inside the chicken into a bowl. Spoon off the fat and blot what remains away with a paper towel, and you can have your chicken with a somewhat lighter heart.

The trick about roasting chicken is to baste constantly. This is a boring chore but well worth the effort. I often like to squeeze the juice of half a lemon over my chicken toward the end, and I roast for at least two hours. I never think in terms of time per pound. A chicken has to be in the oven at least two hours is my motto. When the leg bone wiggles and the skin is the color of teak, it's time to eat.

After you have roasted your chicken you have two wonderful leftovers to look forward to: a chicken sandwich and chicken broth.

A chicken sandwich is a mood elevator. If they were served in prisons, people would commit felonies to get in. A proper chicken sandwich makes a person feel like an indulged child and a sophisticated adult at the same time. With a glass of beer, a glass of wine, or a glass of milk or iced tea, a chicken sandwich makes you feel as if you were sitting in a sunlit tea room at the beginning of spring. Of course, if you are going to feel this way, you must be restrained in your consumption of roast chicken, so you can have half an untouched breast for your sandwich.

A well-made chicken sandwich takes hours to prepare. First of all, you must roast your chicken, but second of all you must make a loaf of bread, the cakey kind of white bread with butter and milk in the dough as well as a little wheat germ. French bread will not do. You want loaf bread, and it is not easy to find a good white loaf these days. Then of course you must make homemade mayonnaise, but many people get around these hurdles by buying bread at the baker's and tarting up prepared mayonnaise with lemon juice.

Slice the white meat thin. Spread the bread with mayonnaise and scatter upon it a dusting of celery salt or ground celery seed. Some people like an open sandwich and some prefer a lid, but in any case it is traditional to trim the crusts—this is a matter of taste. On the other hand, toast is not a matter of taste. A chicken sandwich on toast is not in my opinion a true chicken sandwich.

Now take the chicken carcass and any gravy you have left, plus any of the roasted vegetables as well as any other bird bones you happen to have around (organized types often keep these in the freezer for this purpose). Add filtered water to come three-quarters of the way up and simmer for three hours. Then strain and keep overnight.

The fat that solidifies on top makes a nice airtight lid if you are not going to use the broth for a day or so, but if broth is not in your immediate future, skim off the fat and put it in the freezer (it is easier and less messy to get the fat off at this stage).

This stock, which will turn to jelly in the fridge, is the basis for millions of good soups, but a very quick soup, loved by adults and children (by this I mean my husband and child) is known in our house as

Hen Soup

1. Dice 1 medium potato, 1 small carrot, and 1 scallion or yellow onion. Put these in a pot with a scattering of lima beans or peas. You can add any other vegetable you like. Zucchini and celery are very nice in this soup.
2. Spoon in enough stock to float the vegetables and simmer. About 10 minutes before serving, break up some spaghetti. A nice addition is the tomato-and-basil-flavored spaghetti made by the Prince company and very hard to find. Drop the spaghetti in and let simmer.
3. Add a few drops of lemon juice and a pinch each of pepper and celery salt.
4. If you have any leftover chicken you can dice it up and put it in, too.

This, of course, makes a perfect lunch when accompanied by your perfect chicken sandwich.

The Glory of Chutney

Shortly after I began my career as an amateur jam maker, I decided to try my hand at chutney. My theory was that with these two products in supply I would never have to go Christmas shopping again.

Jam is anxiety-producing. Will it set? And will it set enough, or will it be too runny for most Americans, who prefer a firm jam? As you stare into the preserving pan at your once-huge mass of fruit cooking down, you also wonder if you will have *enough* to give away.

But chutney is a more laid-back proposition. It does not need to set in the way that jam does or to be so closely watched. Chutney is also forgiving. If you don't have currants, use raisins or diced dried fruit of any sort. Dried hot red pepper flakes may be used instead of cayenne. Heavenly batches of the stuff are often the result of such substitutions. Furthermore, the end product is composed of things that do not have to be in exact amounts. For people who only step into the kitchen to fool around once in a great while, chutney is the ticket: Practically foolproof, it is always good and hard to ruin. There is nothing like a homemade condiment, and, besides, you will never have to buy another bottle of wine to take to a dinner party.

My first time out, I made pear chutney (see "In Praise of Pears") from *The Penguin Book of Jams, Pickles and Chutneys* by David and Rose Mabey. The chutney was a huge success. After making it about a dozen times, with all different kinds of pears, I got the basic idea: Add cut-up fruit to salt, brown sugar, pepper, garlic, and vinegar, cook the mixture down, and you will have chutney—just as water, flour, yeast, and salt will produce bread. The matter is simply one of proportions. Always remember, if you want to spend the money you can buy the jam of your dreams, but chutney is idiosyncratic and can only be tailor-made at home.

Some people like their chutney hot, and some prefer it sweet. I myself fell in love with Aeroplane Brand Lime Chutney. I bought it at an Indian spice store because I liked the look of the bottle, which was tall and slender and made of thick, blue-green glass. I had no idea what the contents would taste like, but I soon fell in love with the chutney, too: It was hot, sweet, and suave. One day this product just vanished off the face of the earth; not one single Indian shop carried it. I realized that I would have to attempt to reproduce the recipe in my own kitchen.

And so now, every other month or so, I roll up my sleeves and turn out four jars of lemon or lime chutney. Lemon is closer to what I am looking for, because the lemon rind becomes tender and rather melting, whereas American limes tend to remain somewhat tough and biting.

Making this chutney is a two-day process. The first day, cut up the lemons into little pieces and marinate them overnight in salt. The next day, assemble your spices, pull out the largest kettle you have, and get to work. The recipe is based on one found in *Food as Presents* by Patricia Holden White, but it incorporates elements from Jennifer Brennan's *Curries and Bugles: A Memoir and a Cookbook of the British Raj* (one of the great cookbooks of all time) and the lovely *Carved Angel Cookery Book* (from the Carved Angel restaurant in Devon and available only in England) by Joyce Molyneaux.

Remember that chutney is versatile in the extreme. One ingredient can always be switched for another, and, as you go along, experiment until you get the desired result. Often the cook fears that he or she will never be able to replicate a particularly magnificent batch, but don't worry: The next lot may be even better. I recommend the purchase of a small notebook to keep track of what you do each time.

Lemon Chutney

1. Remove the zest from 8 lemons (about 2½ pounds) with a vegetable peeler, being careful not to include the pith, or white part. Cut away the pith, discard it, and with a knife chop the zest and the flesh as fine as you can. Mix the lemon with 2 tablespoons salt and let the mixture stand in an earthenware or glass bowl overnight.

2. The next day transfer the lemon to a preserving pan or kettle. Add 4 big garlic cloves, minced, ½ cup dried currants (or 1 cup raisins), ½ cup fresh lemon juice, ½ cup cider vinegar, 1 tablespoon grated fresh ginger,

½ teaspoon cayenne, 1 teaspoon each ground cardamom and crushed coriander (use whole coriander seeds and crush them yourself), and ½ teaspoon dried hot red pepper flakes. Stir in a 1-pound box brown sugar and cook the mixture gently over moderate heat, stirring, until it becomes thick.

Cooking down the chutney can take up to 45 minutes, but it is pleasant, restful work. The house smells wonderful, and, while keeping an eye on the stove, you can tuck the telephone under your chin and chat with a loved one, or daydream, or listen to the radio. As you are stirring, boil four 8-ounce jars, jar lids, and gaskets in a large pot of water on a back burner. When you are ready to pack your chutney, take the jars out of the water with tongs and fill them with the chutney. I've found a wide-mouth funnel to be of great assistance in this endeavor, but a ladle works well, too. Smack on the lids, screw on the gaskets, and put the jars back in the boiling water, adding more water if necessary to cover the jars by 2 inches, for a final 10-minute sterilization.

Then remove the jars and leave them in a nice row to remind yourself of what a wonderful person you are. (One of the incidental joys of chutney and jam making is label design: This I leave to my daughter, who started when she was five and does a brilliant job.)

This chutney should not be eaten right away but should sit around for a month or so to ripen. After six months of ripening, it enters into another realm, and no words do justice to the flavor.

Now that you've made chutney, what are you going to do with it? I do not come from chutney-eating people, and my experience of it—prior to my making it at home—was as an integral accompaniment to Indian food in Indian restaurants.

Lately I have branched out. This condiment, user-friendly to the cook, is user-friendly to the eater as well. Nothing beats it with plain baked salmon. Chutney is also divine with roast chicken, hot or cold, or with cold meat of any kind. It is nice with cold vegetables, especially potatoes. Some people like it on bread with cream cheese, and I was once given, at a fancy party, a tiny peanut butter and chutney sandwich that was delicious.

And, when no one is looking, it is perfectly all right to open a jar, dip in a spoon, and eat the chutney straight—in the name of culinary science and art, of course—just to see if you got it right.

Halloween

As every parent knows, children are great traditionalists. All you need do is set something in motion and you will find yourself doing it the same way, year after year after year. Psychologists say this is good for us. The things that keep mankind going—ritual, stability, routine—are beginning to fray, and we are all the worse for it.

No matter what else happens in October, Halloween is still the big deal. Therefore, if I forget to buy that nasty, synthetic woolly stuff that one tacks to windows to look like fake cobwebs, chaos reigns. My daughter likes the same thing, year after year after year, and I must confess that I do, too.

On Halloween the parents in our neighborhood dress up their precious angels and form a parade, complete with flashlights and homemade noisemakers, and march around the General Theological Seminary. Afterward people must be taken home and fed, usually the same thing that you fed them last year.

I don't mind admitting that I have never liked pumpkin. I hate pumpkin pie and am lukewarm about pumpkin soup. I once had an unhappy encounter with a stew served in a pumpkin: It did not further endear pumpkin to me. I have bought cheese pumpkins as well as "pie" or "sweetie pie" pumpkins. These are pale orange, dense fleshed, not a bit stringy, and not to be used for jack-o'-lanterns. I have steamed them and baked them and fried them. I have dotted them with butter and brown sugar and scattered them with garlic and cheese, and I still say it's pumpkin and to hell with it.

Children, however, seem to require something pumpkin-like on the table at Halloween *even if they don't eat it*. For them I recommend butternut or acorn squash split, seeded, and baked with butter and brown sugar. The seeds, of course, go into a colander with the seeds from the jack-o'-lantern to be endlessly washed and separated from any pumpkin or squash sludge, then drained, salted, and roasted. When you serve these before or after dinner, even adults will tell you how delicious they are.

For grown-ups, I suggest the pumpkin tian in John Thorne's noble and mighty *Simple Cooking*. John Thorne, who lives in Maine, puts out a newsletter of the same name that is enchanting, opinionated, and full of good things. The pumpkin tian, in addition to being one of the most delicious things you will ever eat, demonstrates that the whole is more magnificent than the sum of its meager parts. The first time I made this dish I almost collapsed at the realization that something so easy could taste so wonderful.

My version of the recipe calls for either butternut or delicata squash or a combination of the two. For Squash Tian, proportions aren't the issue, method is; but for 4 people you probably need about 2 big butternuts or 4 of the sweeter, medium-sized delicatas. Peel, seed, and cut the squash into 1-inch chunks. Shake the chunks in a bag of flour, shaking off the excess flour, and put them into an oiled or buttered shallow baking dish. Scatter the squash with about ⅓ cup of good Parmesan; 1 large garlic clove, minced; and pepper to taste. Drizzle the tian with about ¼ to ⅓ cup best olive oil and put it into a *preheated* 400° F. oven. The oven must be really hot, or instead of a crispy-topped, melting ("molten," John Thorne says) dish you will end up with a sodden mess—trust me, I have had this happen. Bake the tian for 30 to 40 minutes. I myself would be very happy to eat this with a salad, but as we do not necessarily live by vegetables alone, something else must be provided—especially if you provided it last year.

I recommend Meat Loaf, which is good hot, cold, or at room temperature and can be made in advance. It is nice, homey food and usually a hit with old and young.

I love meat loaf of any kind. Like potato salad, it always seems to be good. I have never run into an unlovable meat loaf, but I have loved some better than others. A few years ago I ran into a really delicious meat loaf at Cadwell's Corner, the premier breakfast and lunch place in West Cornwall, Connecticut. This meat loaf's winning feature is its texture, which is light and velvety. Naturally I attempted to prize out of David Cadwell (an agreeable, bearded former coffee buyer and father of twins) the secret of his success, which actually may be that of his wife, Alice. The trick is to soak two 1-inch-thick slices of homemade bread (crusts discarded) in 1 cup buttermilk for 20 minutes and stir the mixture into 2 pounds ground chuck with 2 large eggs. The Cadwells make their own bread, but any good grainy loaf, such as *levain,* will do. Perfectionists can buy a round loaf—about 7 inches in diameter and about 3 inches high—and cut 2 slices from the middle. (In a pinch, 2 slices of the best packaged bread you can find will do.)

It doesn't matter how you season the meat loaf: Every cook has a different method. I use 1 large garlic clove, minced; 1 tablespoon

Dijon-style mustard; 1 teaspoon Worcestershire sauce; and 1 tablespoon ketchup. Sometimes I add a couple of tablespoons of a nice
thing called Ortolina, which tastes rather like a concentrated form
of V8 vegetable juice. You can buy it in a tube or a jar in specialty
foods shops. Bake the meat loaf in a loaf pan, 9 by 5 by 3 inches,
at 350° F. for about 1 hour.

The bread and buttermilk combination makes this meat loaf
light and springy. If you keep kosher, rich chicken stock would
probably work as well as buttermilk.

After a green salad, the children will want dessert.

Of course, you have stayed up the night before decorating a
spiderweb cake. I made this one year and have not been permitted to stop. It is any old cake decorated with orange icing using
the fine nib of the cake-decorating kit (the one you write "Happy
Birthday" with) in a spiderweb design. And because you have been
a good person and have bought the nasty, synthetic woolly stuff
that makes fake cobwebs, you also have a black plastic spider (it
comes in the package) to put on your cake. That is, unless you are
amazingly energetic and have decided to create your own spider
out of icing, which can be done by anyone possessing paste food
coloring and a field guide.

But what kind of cake? My vote is for something called Wensley cake, a recipe from a now-defunct cooking magazine. (It is a
sad fact of my life that many of my best recipes come from now-
defunct sources.)

A Wensley cake is meant to have a layer of Wensleydale cheese.
I have made it this way, and although I thought it was delicious,
my family found it weird. Made without cheese it is just plain
delicious.

Wensley Cake

1. Beat together 2 sticks butter and 1 cup brown sugar.
2. Beat in 4 lightly beaten large eggs.
3. Stir in 2 cups all-purpose flour, 1 teaspoon baking powder, 1 teaspoon ground ginger, and ¼ teaspoon each of mace, ground cloves, and cinnamon.
4. Stir in 1 cup golden raisins (dried cherries are a *very* nice substitute if you're lucky enough to have some), 1¼ cups currants, 1 cup dark raisins, 1 cup grated apple, and the grated zest of 1 orange. Mix well.
5. Bake the cake in a buttered 8-inch round cake pan (2 inches deep) lined with parchment paper in the middle of a preheated 375° F. oven for 25 minutes. Reduce the heat to 325° F. and bake for 1 hour more, checking the cake from time to time. It is done when a skewer comes out with some crumbs adhering to it.

The cake, wrapped in wax paper and stored in a tin, improves after a few days and keeps well if you happen to have any left. This nice, old-fashioned dessert has a lot of depth to it. In fact, the whole meal has a lot of depth to it—a cheering supper on a spooky night, usually right after daylight saving time disappears and the sky gets dark around 4:30.

Last year our children marched happily around the block, and the minute they got inside a torrential storm broke. A ten-year-old neighbor appeared wearing a gorilla suit and a terrifying mask with little red eyes that blinked, and although he kept taking off his mask and saying, "Don't be scared! I'm Robert Jordan!" my daughter and her friends remained in a state of exhausted petrifaction.

Then my husband appeared, having been pelted with eggs and almost mugged by some overzealous teens. The rain beat down, Robert's mask was taken off for good, my husband's jacket was put in the washing machine, and after dinner not a crumb was left.

Turkey Angst

There are times when I am led to believe that I am the only person in the United States who truly likes the taste of turkey—plain old roast turkey that the next day provides plain old turkey sandwiches to be spread with Russian dressing.

So many other people seem to dread turkey. The highest expression of this loathing can be found under "Turkey Remains and How to Inter Them with Numerous Scarce Recipes," in the "Nonsense and Stray Phrases" section of the posthumous collection of F. Scott Fitzgerald's writings titled *The Crack-up.* "This is one of the most useful recipes," he writes, "for, though not 'chic,' it tells us what to do with turkey after the holiday, and how to extract the most value from it. Take the remnants, or, if they have been consumed, take the various plates on which the turkey or its parts have rested and stew them for two hours in milk of magnesia. Stuff with moth-balls." This is the sort of thing that gives turkey a bad name.

In my opinion the poor turkey is a mere scapegoat for the mire of conflicted feelings flooding our psyches at holiday time. It is hard to divorce the turkey from the expectations of the family table, the sibling rivalries, the unspoken resentments, the secret rages that occur even in the happiest families. Add to this the exhaustion of travel or the exhaustion of preparing to welcome traveling relatives, and even the juiciest, tenderest turkey may be as sawdust. Of course, it is possible in the most harmonious family to produce a turkey that may as well *be* sawdust, just as it is also possible to produce a magnificent turkey in the middle of a family psychodrama. Either way you slice it, it may be easier to blame the turkey.

But what *about* the turkey, if only because people get it fed to them at least once if not twice a year? My mother believes that a small tom turkey is the best turkey and that instead of increasing the size of your bird you should increase the *number* of them to feed a large party. Eight pounds is about tops in her opinion. To this I would add that if you can get your hands on a real, for-sure, free-range organic turkey the size almost does not matter: It will be the best turkey you ever had. My local health food store purveys organic, free-running Amish turkeys at Thanksgiving, and I have roasted one as large as seventeen pounds. It was sensational.

As to roasting, some people feel that twenty minutes a pound is fine, but I prefer half an hour in a slower oven. I want my turkey to be tender and juicy. The name of that game is *constant basting,* a boring but necessary chore. I dust my bird with paprika and put it in a 400° F. oven for half an hour. Then I cover it with a foil hat and lower the heat to 325° F. Meanwhile, on the back burner is a pot containing chicken stock, turkey giblets, and any other turkey parts lying around plus one onion and a large clove of smashed garlic. A nicer person would throw in the neck, but I am not a nicer person, and I roast the neck, which I then eat all by myself in the kitchen without a trace of guilt, because I did all the work.

Turkey does not need a speck of salt, and if you baste constantly you do not need any fat either. The extra stock will make a heavenly gravy. If there is any left over you can put it in your soup pot or in the fridge (where it will harden into a delicious jelly that can be eaten with a spoon by people like me who like this sort of thing).

Of course the plain fact about turkey is that, no matter how many people sit at your table, you will have leftovers. And after a while people are sick of turkey sandwiches. Furthermore, lots of people really hate turkey soup. Many years ago I was served turkey Tetrazzini, which I vowed I would never, never, never eat again.

If your family hates turkey soup, you can make a rich turkey stock and turn it into *jook,* a Chinese rice gruel (and second cousin to the Cuban *asopao*), after the fashion of my friend Cynthia B. Elitzer, who grew up in Hong Kong. To this rich turkey stock you add a couple of handfuls of rice and cook it down into a savory mess to which you add some chopped turkey. When sprinkled with scallions, drizzled with soy sauce, and spiked with a dash of dark sesame oil, this concoction makes you realize how nice life can be, and it is nourishing, too.

I myself look forward to turning the last bits of turkey into turkey salad. Dice up your leftovers and toss them in a bowl with a little olive oil, salt and pepper, and a dash of lemon juice. Some people like a shake of Tabasco, too. A spoonful of capers, some chopped-up *cornichons,* and minced scallion are admirable additions. You can make up your own mayonnaise or add lemon juice to your favorite bottled variety, then mix it into the turkey. On a nice bed of greens this makes a yummy lunch. You need not feel greedy if this turkey salad is consumed entirely by you. A person who bastes a turkey all day long on behalf of other people's holiday pleasure deserves it. This person is a *saint,* and if she or he has finished off all the nicest turkey bits plus the last of the capers, tough darts. Turkey roasting's heroes deserve rewards.

Some years ago, the turkey producers of this country got together to figure out how to lure Americans into consuming turkey at times other than Thanksgiving and Christmas. They came up with the idea of selling turkey breasts, because they are less cumbersome than the whole bird, less labor-intensive to cook, and easier to store, and also because many people prefer white meat.

I have cooked a couple of these, and, although they certainly will feed a number of people, something—apart from the rest of the turkey—is missing. There is a *je ne sais quoi* about turkey cooking—the air of festivity, the family squabbles, the constant basting—that does not apply to turkey breast, which is, really, a convenience food. You barely have to baste it, and you don't get any of those nice parts like the pope's nose or the neck to keep for yourself. It is turkey devoid of drama—the highs and lows of dark and white meat, the legs to fight over, the carcass to pick over.

And there you have it. Although turkey is delicious in itself, it is burdened with *context,* as they say in the literary criticism racket. A turkey without seasonal angst is like a baseball game without the national anthem, a winter without snow, a birthday party without candles. For better and worse the exhaustion, the exhilaration, the expectations, and the complications are a kind of emotional condiment, the secret element that gives turkey its essential spirit.

All the Trimmings

Aside from your initial ride on a two-wheeler or solo outing as a licensed driver, there is nothing as liberating as the first Thanksgiving dinner you organize entirely on your own.

This year, you say to yourself, we will *not* have those nasty creamed onions. And I will not put gingersnaps into the chestnuts, and we will not have prunes in the stuffing. This time I will do it *my* way.

All cooks who have spent their holidays in the households of others long for their chance to take charge of a festive meal. It is rather like the redecoration of a family home. Out go the dusty, spotted, faded upholstery fabric and the stiff chair no one ever sits in. The old rugs are sent out to be cleaned, and the walls are stripped of their dingy paper. What you want is *your* stamp on things.

My own first Thanksgiving featured a controversial unstuffed turkey. What I was after was a simplified, elegant meal, a table you could get up from feeling fresh and light instead of weighted down. I did not want four desserts; I wanted one, with oranges and toasted walnuts to be served with coffee. My first time out was a big success, and I felt as if I had not only reinvented the wheel but painted it a color no one had ever thought of before.

But the inevitable truth is that after you have done this a number of times your liberated meal becomes the standard issue; and, if you deviate in the slightest, people are bound to notice and whine, "What? No corn-bread stuffing? No ginger cake? Aren't you going to have the toasted walnuts?" And so forth.

The linchpin of Thanksgiving is the turkey. People have complicated feelings about turkey, but I am proud to stand up and testify that I love it. Moreover, I ardently wish that the turkey growers of America would breed *down*. What I want is a small, organic turkey that feeds six without several years' worth of leftovers. But until that day comes I will make do cooking a large turkey.

The real emotional issue is the stuffing. People feel about stuffing the way they feel about their childhood toys. They do not like change or surprises. What they are after is comfort and stability.

For years I made a corn-bread and prosciutto stuffing that everyone adored but that, unfortunately, I got tired of. So I set about experimenting. Stuffings are *fun*, after all. It is interesting to make them up and try them out.

Last year, with a large can of peeled chestnuts on hand and a box of pecans sent by a Southern friend, I set to work. I myself hate a sweet or weird stuffing, and those recipes that contain oysters, figs, and Port are not for me. I like a straightforward, nutty, savory stuffing. This one contained the pecans, sautéed in olive oil and butter; the chestnuts, which were added to the pecans as they cooked; a minced garlic clove; two chopped scallions; and a bag of white-bread stuffing. The mixture was then moistened with chicken stock and stuffed into the bird.

Although it was gratifying that not a morsel remained, I was left with nothing for breakfast. I come from a family that likes leftovers the morning after, and I was *so* looking forward to a cup of hot coffee and a plate of nice, cold stuffing. I was consoled only by the fact that I had hit upon a stuffing I would be happy with for several years.

For a long time I was addicted to baked Brussels sprouts as a side dish, but then my attention wandered. Subsequently, in a book entitled *America Eats* by William Woys Weaver (Harper & Row), which is subtitled *Forms of Edible Folk Art,* I found a recipe I fell in love with: a dish from Colonial New Jersey, which, like Parma and York, used to be a center for fine hams.

This recipe—referred to by me as Parsnips and Ham, the reverse order from the original, because my version is more vegetable than meat—handsomely takes the place of baked sweet potatoes and gives guests a thrill. Put 6 cups lightly steamed julienned parsnips (about 2 pounds) into a buttered dish; scatter them with 2 ounces of the best ham you can find, ½ cup when diced up; and cover everything with 1 cup of a plain béchamel sauce to which some Dijon-style mustard has been added. Bake this in a 400° F. oven until it bubbles (20 minutes or so), sprinkle it with fresh parsley, bring the dish to the table, and make all your guests ecstatic.

As I browsed through *America Eats,* which is full of other wonderful recipes and gorgeous pictures, something else caught my eye—and the eye of my daughter, then aged five. It was a recipe for cider jelly, a beautiful Victorian dessert. If you have an ornamental pudding mold, this is the recipe to use it with.

Cider Jelly

1. In a bowl mix 5 packets unflavored gelatin with 2 cups sugar (or less, to taste), the grated zest of 1 lemon, and ¼ teaspoon cinnamon. Over this pour 1 cup cold water and stir to combine well.
2. Add the juice of 2 lemons, or about ⅓ cup.
3. Bring 1 quart apple cider to a boil, skimming off any scum. Pour the cider into the gelatin mixture and stir until the gelatin is completely dissolved. Set aside to cool.
4. When the mixture is cooled but not yet set, pour it into a 1-quart mold and chill it in the refrigerator overnight, or until set.

This jelly looks perfectly glorious and can be either an alternative or an accompaniment to the traditional cranberry sauce. It is not only novel but also delicious.

But back to my Thanksgiving veggies. Finally I longed for something fresh. I served steamed broccoli, plain for the children. For the grown-ups I spiced it up—you can call it Spicy Broccoli. The preparation is simple: Steam 1 large bunch of broccoli until really tender and then heat up about ¼ cup olive oil to which you add 1 large garlic clove, minced, plus ¼ teaspoon (or more) hot red pepper flakes. Then arrange the broccoli on a platter and drizzle the oil on top. It is the easiest thing in the world. If I lived alone I would eat it for all three meals. This broccoli is not traditional—at least it is not traditional to anyone I know—but it is a perfect contrast to all that baked stuff you get at Thanksgiving—fresh, snappy, and green.

• • •

A big salad and something nice for dessert bring to an end this festive meal, along with coffee, oranges, and toasted walnuts. At the
City and Country School Fall Fair in Greenwich Village, I recently
bought a jar of toasted walnuts made by one of the parents, a singer
by the name of Linda Langford. They were so wonderful I called her
up and begged for the recipe, which she had found, it turned out,
in *The Pink Adobe Cookbook* by Rosalea Murphy (Dell Publishing).

Rosemary Walnuts

1. Melt 2½ tablespoons unsalted butter with 2 teaspoons
   dried rosemary (crumbled), 1 teaspoon salt, and ½ teaspoon cayenne.
2. Pour this mixture over 2 cups walnuts, tossing to coat
   them.
3. Bake the nuts on a cookie sheet at 350° F. for 10 minutes.

I made pounds of these walnuts, thinking I would be able to
keep some for myself, but the instant they reached the table they
were gone. The trick about this recipe is that *you can never make
enough*. And, furthermore, a savory at the end of a meal provides
the perfect finishing touch.

This menu is now my tradition, but I know that in not too
long a time my daughter will grow up and decide that it is *her* turn,
and we will travel to her household for Thanksgiving. And there I
will find the traditional meal, totally renovated and redesigned: the
beginning—for that is the way these things go—of a new tradition.

Condiments

Variety, as we are told, is the spice of life, and as for the spice of life in the kitchen, condiments are the name of the game.

Imagine a kitchen without mustard, ketchup, or Worcestershire sauce: Here is a kitchen in which you can't make a decent Welsh rabbit or shepherd's pie. Imagine life without dill pickles, corn relish, chutney, or pickled okra.

I myself am hipped on a number of condiments without which I would not dream of cooking. This shows me to be a politically correct and multicultural person. After all, to cook without stepping out of your own country is boring, the sort of culinary equivalent of reading only what are now called DWEMs—dead white European males.

And so in a spirit of cultural inquiry and multicultural appreciation, in a broad-based, bias-free, brotherly and sisterly modality (so to speak), I open my pantry.

My life would be totally impoverished without lime pickle, a fiery Indian concoction that contains everything I love: It is very, very hot, salty, and extremely tart. Many people find it inedible, but I adore it, and so do many of my friends. There are numerous brands in any Indian specialty store, but I stick by Bedekar's Lime Pickle, and I have been through jars and jars of it. It is a deep, lethal-looking orange and contains limes preserved in salt and hot chili pepper, a perfect thing to serve as a spicy note with leftover cold beef or chicken or baked salmon, with which it is *amazing*. I have never found a way to use lime pickle other than as a condiment, but I am happy with it. A little lime pickle makes steamed vegetables light up. You can mix it with yogurt and serve it with steamed vegetables or cold squash. Once you taste it it becomes a craving . . . at least in my house.

I have not been without fermented black beans since I first encountered them years ago in a dish of shrimp in black bean sauce. These are pungent little beans preserved with salt and ginger. You can buy them in bags at Chinese grocery stores, and they are very cheap, or you can sometimes find them packed in jars at fancy grocery stores, in which case they are more expensive. Whichever way you buy them (and if you buy them in bags, it is wise to decant them into glass) they are worth it, since they have endless uses.

They are heavenly in vegetable pastas: Chopped-up cauliflower or broccoli sautéed in olive oil and garlic and sprinkled with some fermented black beans on top of *linguine* is fast, easy, and totally delicious. This basic method works well with any kind of vegetable, including eggplant, which has a deep affinity with pasta. You can use them as an interesting substitute for capers and sprinkle them on top of *focaccia* or homemade pizza.

As for capers, watching my daughter digging out the capers from the caper jar with an iced tea spoon makes me realize that heredity plays a large part in one's taste in food. As a small child I happily polished off jar after jar of cocktail onions; then I graduated to capers. My daughter started on capers at around age three and demanded that they be put into her tuna fish (a delicious addition). I like them in black butter on salmon or skate or brains, but I am not permitted to order brains when I am out and I would never dream of cooking them at home.

When we were courting, my husband once took me for my birthday to a fancy restaurant where I ordered brains in black butter, and when they were served, he refused to look at me as I ate them and turned to stare at a group of strangers who were sitting to his left, even though he and I were side by side on a banquette. (He also refused to watch me eat a plate of squid in its own ink at a cheap Cuban-Chinese restaurant.)

Capers are a wonderful addition to *ratatouille,* to pizza, and to rice salad made with diced Swiss cheese, onions, and scallions. If you mash them up with cream cheese, celery salt, and some paprika you will have made a cheese spread that is either Viennese or Hungarian or both, and very delicious. As a little girl I used to get my celery sticks stuffed with this delicious mixture, and I once made it to cater an opening for a painter pal, and it was gone in a flash, although two guests, one Hungarian and the other of German Jewish descent, argued over precisely where it came from. As for my daughter, she feels that capers should either go into the tuna fish or be eaten straight from the jar.

A long time ago, the much-missed *Seven Days* magazine called Thai red curry paste "the best food you can buy in a can." I do not recommend this to anyone who does not like things *hot.* This stuff is *fire.* It is also delicious and a surefire cure for colds, flu, and general weakness.

The ingredients include chili, garlic, shrimp paste, lemon-grass, *galanga,* and salt. Since I am not an expert at Thai food, I only use this stuff one way, but I use it often. I put 1 tablespoon of paste into a quart of chicken stock plus the juice of 1 or 2 lemons. When it is hot, I ladle it into a bowl and spoon in about a cup of jasmine rice and some scallions. You need to drink large quantities of water with this, but it is good for you, I swear it.

I am also dependent on something called *gomasio* (available at the health food store), which is a Japanese condiment made of toasted sesame seeds and salt. Usually this is the only saltlike thing available at a macrobiotic restaurant and a very good thing it is. It is lovely on baked chicken, or added to the flour you are going to coat your chicken in before you fry it. It is nice on steamed or sautéed vegetables or buttered toast. It makes a delicious salad dressing with buttermilk or yogurt. You can make it yourself and control the amount of salt plus the fineness of the sesame seeds. Some *gomasio* is grainy, some is powdery. I like mine grainy, the seeds very toasted.

Recently I received a copy of a book called *Sophie's Table* by Sophie Grigson (daughter of the late, great Jane). This book contains all manner of wonderful things, and the fact that it is not available in this country (it was published by Michael Joseph Ltd. in London) is another example of America's decline. In it there is a recipe for something that is now referred to as Condiment, but its real name is *Dukka*. It is an Egyptian spice powder (a recipe can be found in Claudia Roden's *A Book of Middle Eastern Food*). I'm sure it has many uses, but I must confess that I eat it right out of the jar. I must also confess that I am totally addicted to it.

Dukka

In a skillet toast 1 ounce hazelnuts, 4 tablespoons sesame seeds, 2 tablespoons coriander seeds, 1½ tablespoons whole cumin seeds, ½ tablespoon black peppercorns, 2 teaspoons ground cinnamon, and ½ tablespoon salt. Grind the mixture in the blender.

After a while you can mess around with this recipe. Caught without hazelnuts I used walnuts, which give it a kind of buttery texture, and now I use a combination of walnuts and hazelnuts. I have used more or less pepper, ground cumin, fewer sesame seeds. I have sprinkled this on buttered toast, on poached eggs, and served it in a saltcellar to sprinkle on rice.

I introduced this to my sister last summer. I gave her a taste, and an hour later I caught her in the kitchen eating it out of the jar with a spoon: These things obviously run in families.

And there you have it: the things that brighten up your kitchen and add a little surprise to ordinary dishes. Some people keep Moroccan preserved lemons, or fermented bean curd, or English pickled walnuts. But give me some fermented black beans, a jar of capers, and my adored condiment, and I can turn the plainest steamed zucchini into something else: its elemental self sprung magically into some more charming guise, which is what the spice of life, after all, is all about.

Wonderful Lentil Soup

In all your life you will be hard-pressed to find something as simple, soothing, and forgiving, as consoling as lentil soup. You can take things out of it or put things into it. It can be fancy or plain, and it will never let you down.

There are two ways to make it: healthy and unhealthy. Amazingly enough, both are delicious. Furthermore you can purée it or leave it alone, and you can eat it hot or cold.

The unhealthy way is made with slab bacon, preferably double-smoked, cut into dice and sautéed with onion and garlic. Or made with short ribs, which have a sublime flavor and tons of fat, most of which is happily absorbed by the lentils and then passed right into your bloodstream. You can throw in some delicious, high-calorie, and very indigestible sausage. All of these will produce a delicious soup.

Or you can poach your lentils gently in a very rich, defatted chicken or beef stock, then pour the result in a blender with a spike of brandy (or not) and some cayenne pepper and serve this velvety potion to grown-ups.

You can simmer your soup with tomatoes and red peppers, or

you can leave it alone in some water with a few vegetables. Even this abstemious preparation tastes fine. The fact is, lentils always taste fine, and if you hate soup you can poach them, drain them, and turn them into a salad.

But it is soup that concerns us here for a number of reasons: It is warming, comforting, good for you, and most important *it is easy.* It is *thrillingly* easy, and it has a quality loved by all pressed cooks—it does the work for you.

Lentils are friendly—the Miss Congeniality of the bean world. They take well to almost anything. But let us start from scratch. The most minimal lentil soup calls for a cup of lentils; a quart of water or stock of any kind; one sliced carrot; one or two cloves of garlic, minced; one small diced onion; and there you are. This makes a nice plain soup to which no hungry person can object.

The next step is to add to this one potato, diced up (I love lentil soup with potatoes in it), one rib of celery, one bay leaf, a sprig of thyme, another clove of garlic, and you have a more varied *potage* that is actually a vegetable soup with lentils.

Going one step further, string beans and lentil soup seem to call out to each other. You can add this to your vegetable soup with lentils or simply make lentil and string bean soup with garlic and onions. A tablespoon of tomato paste goes well with any of these combinations.

A purée of lentil soup with chopped spinach is heaven, spiked with a little cream or yogurt. And a piping hot lentil soup with some long-cooked, very tender broccoli di rape mixed in is divine (for those who adore broccoli di rape, which is pungent, bitter, and full of wonderful flavor). The bliss of this all is that, aside from a little vegetable chopping, *there is almost nothing to do.*

You cook this gently on the stove. You will have soup in an

hour. You will have a better soup if you wait a little longer. You will have a slightly different soup if you add some cut-up tomatoes, tomato paste, or some leftover canned tomatoes. The point is, You can't mess it up. Lentil soup comes through for you. With a loaf of bread, a salad, and some cheese, and something or other for dessert, you have your midday or evening meal without much trouble on your part.

But what if you want a nice, rich, slightly unhealthy soup? Or you would like to take a lot of trouble?

In the first case you can dice up some double-smoked bacon, sauté with the vegetables, and add a few veal bones. Add the lentils and cook for a long, long time. If you want to go the distance, use veal bones and a short rib, sawed into pieces by the butcher. Make sure the veal bones have lots of marrow. This produces a rich, thick, velvety soup but nothing you want to give to vegetarians or people on fat-free diets. Still, once a year it is a truly splendid soup.

And now if you would like to take a little trouble with your soup you can pick up a copy of *An Invitation to Indian Cooking* by Madhur Jaffrey or *Curries and Bugles: A Memoir and a Cookbook of the British Raj* by Jennifer Brennan and concoct Mulligatawny Soup.

I confess that I have never made this soup, although I have always wanted to, but it is not the sort of thing I feel I could get my family to eat. The two books mentioned above are two of my standbys: I *love* these books, and since every single thing I have ever cooked out of either has been totally delicious, I can guarantee that this soup, a blend of the two recipes, will turn out swell.

Mulligatawny Soup

1. Put 2 cloves garlic, one 1-inch piece of peeled ginger, 1 onion (chopped), 1 teaspoon cayenne pepper, 1 teaspoon turmeric, 1 teaspoon ground coriander, and one bay leaf, broken up into a blender and purée.
2. Put 3 tablespoons oil in a saucepan and bring to moderate heat. Add the garlic-ginger-onion paste and fry, stirring, for about 3 minutes.
3. Add the diced meat from 4 chicken thighs or the diced meat from 2 chicken breasts. Stir for 1 minute. Add 1 quart chicken stock. (Jennifer Brennan's recipe calls for 6 fluid ounces coconut milk; Madhur Jaffrey's, which calls for lamb, leaves out the coconut milk. Jennifer Brennan also calls for tamarind paste, and Madhur Jaffrey calls for lemon juice. I am on the side of convenience and am leaving out the tamarind and the coconut milk, which may be hard to find.)
4. Add 6 tablespoons of lentils and let the soup simmer, covered, for about 30 minutes. Fifteen minutes before the soup is done, add 3 tablespoons rice.
5. Strain out the meat and purée the soup. Put it back in the pot and add 1 tablespoon lemon juice. To serve sprinkle the top with *garam masala* or chopped scallions.

This constitutes a festive dish which can also be made without meat or meat stock and served to vegetarians. For background you need a freezing drizzle, a dark sky, a fire in the fireplace if you have one, a cozily set table, and perhaps a nice, friendly, all-American cheese popover to go with this Indian soup. You need some hungry friends and some baked apples for dessert.

This is the sort of soup that warms you up and keeps you warm, but then, all lentil soups are like that, bless their little hearts.

How to Face the Holidays

When Thanksgiving has passed and the leaves are off the trees, the harried modern person looks to the winter holidays like someone slumped across a railroad track contemplating an oncoming train.

No matter of what persuasion you may be, the idea of Hanukkah or Christmas with New Year's Eve to follow is enough to fill the most cheerful heart with dread: shopping, wrapping, hiding presents, going to the post office and standing on line forever, trying to get a taxi in the freezing cold to bring home the ingredients for a festive meal, and so forth.

The older I get, the more I shrink from the frenzy and hype and the potlatch aspect of present giving. I yearn for some simpler time when people gave each other jars of homemade jam and hand-knitted mittens.

Lately I have begun to think less of *holiday* and have turned my attention instead to the idea of *winter*, of trying to fill the house with good things to feed the unexpected guests who always turn up. I want to make a gesture toward that longed-for simpler time by producing something that is made only once a year. After several seasons of trial and error, I have found two splendid things. They look daunting but are actually easy. There is nothing else like them. They must be made by hand. And they cannot be bought.

Both of these items come from English cookbooks. One is the Country Christmas Cake from Jane Grigson's *English Food,* a book I could not live without, and the other is the Spiced Beef for Christmas from Elizabeth David's *Spices, Salt and Aromatics in the English Kitchen.* (The latter recipe was also reprinted in her *Omelette and a Glass of Wine.*) Although these are classic Christmas recipes, they can be enjoyed by anyone who is not, in the case of the beef, strictly kosher. They are splendid winter foods: rich, cheering, and full of flavor. The act of making them gives a person a proper holiday feeling. The act of eating them makes one realize the limitations of language: *Magnificent, sublime, transcendent* all come to mind but fall short. Both must be fixed in advance. The beef should be prepared ten days before it is to be cooked, and the cake has to be baked in November (October is even better) or very early December and then kept in a tin to mellow.

The only complicated thing about Country Christmas Cake is the list of ingredients. Once these are assembled, the whole thing is, so to speak, a piece of cake.

On a Friday or Saturday night (this is a good cake to make on a weekend when there is a little more time), chop up fine: 2½ pounds mixed raisins, pitted prunes, and dried figs; 2 ounces candied peel; 2 ounces candied cherries; and 3 ounces candied or preserved ginger. Add the grated zests and juices of 1 large orange and 1 large lemon, 1 tablespoon of bitter orange marmalade, and

1 tablespoon of apricot jam. Add 1 cup of stewed apple (applesauce will do) and 2 tablespoons of sweet Sherry. Mix, cover, and leave overnight.

The next day, sift together 3 cups flour and 1 teaspoon each of ground cinnamon, ground ginger, baking powder, nutmeg, ground cloves, and allspice. Cream ½ pound of butter with 1 cup of dark brown sugar until fluffy and beat in 4 eggs, 1 at a time, and 1 teaspoon of vanilla. Mix the fruit and flour alternately into the butter, brown sugar, and eggs.

Line the bottom and side of a deep 10-inch springform pan with 3 layers of parchment and pour in the batter. Bake at 325° F. for 2 hours and then at 300° F. for another 2 hours. If your oven temperature is unstable, check it frequently. Take the cake out of the oven, pierce it all over with a skewer, and pour over it 1 tablespoon whiskey or brandy. Leave it to cool in its pan, then remove it, peel off the parchment, wrap the cake in wax paper, place it in an airtight tin, and leave it in the pantry for at least a month to take care of itself.

When the time comes to decant the cake, it is traditional to glaze it with some nice jelly (I like quince) and cover it with marzipan, which Jane Grigson suggests you make yourself. For beginners, however, the stuff in the 7-ounce tube works fine. Roll it out, cut it to fit, and you will find that it sticks to the cake in a very satisfying fashion.

Although this cake can be served with nothing else on it, it is also traditional to cover the marzipan with royal icing, an easy icing that can be found in any basic cookbook. You frost the cake the day before you eat it. The top layer will get ever so slightly hard and then give under the teeth, and one day's rest will take the intensity of the sweetness from the icing. Last year my daughter and I decorated our cake with swags, marzipan flowers, silver and gold dragées, and sugar crystals. It was quite a sight—a kind of demented-looking pile of icing.

Country Christmas Cake has a rich, deep taste, as complicated as a brocade or tapestry, and makes a person think of those magnificent aged Sauternes. It is suave, intense, and delicious down to the last crumb. Most impressive is the fact that you have made this gorgeous, amazing, traditional cake *yourself* from an ancient recipe. Hands down, it is the best I have ever made—and also the best I have ever eaten. And, because it is so rich, you serve it in tiny slices, so there is lots left over for the deserving cook to enjoy in the afternoon.

And now to the spiced beef. Like all of Elizabeth David's recipes, this one is perfectly expressed, perfectly correct, and perfectly delicious. The fact that *I* produced this rather magnificent thing shocked even me. My mother was also extremely impressed, as were the six friends who gathered on Christmas day and ate every scrap of the beef, which was cut *paper* thin.

This recipe is another example of something that takes just a few minutes' work and pays you back a million times for your meager efforts. That is my idea of heaven: a huge payoff for not too much work.

For Spiced Beef, go to the butcher and get the leanest 6 pounds of bottom round he has. Some supermarkets sell what is called "natural beef," which is grass-fed, slaughtered young, and tested for pesticide residues. If you can find this, or any organic beef, get it.

Take the beef home, put it in a crock with a cover, rub it all over with ½ cup dark brown sugar, and chill it. Rub it with the sugar once a day for two days. Then crush together 1 cup coarse sea salt and ⅓ cup each of black peppercorns, juniper berries, and allspice. Rub the meat with this mixture. Continue to chill it, rubbing and turning it for 10 days. This whole operation takes about 10 seconds per day.

When you are about to cook the beef, wipe off the spices (or keep some of them on, which makes it more pastramilike) and put it in a casserole into which it just fits. Pour in a cup of water, put a piece of wax paper under the lid, and roast the meat at 290° F. for 5 hours.

Leave the beef to cool in the juice. Then take it out, wrap it in wax paper, and put it on a board. Put another board on top of it, weight it with about 5 pounds (cans will do nicely), and chill it overnight. The beef will pack down and can be sliced thin enough to see through. It has, according to Elizabeth David, "a rich, mellow, spicy flavour which does seem to convey to us some sort of idea of the food eaten by our forbears."

These two delicacies have that profound, original, homemade taste that cannot be replicated, no matter what you spend. They make the person who made them feel ennobled. After all, it is holiday time. Aren't we meant to draw together and express our good feelings for one another? What could be better than to offer something so elementally, so wholesomely down-home and yet elegant? And both go a long way: You can feed a lot of loved ones with them.

So this is my way around the holidays. If I did nothing else, I would still make this cake and spiced beef and fill my head with visions of candles and pine boughs. The sun goes down at four o'clock, the air is damp and chill, but in the pantry my cake is mellowing, and soon I will spice my beef as centuries of people have done before me.

Plain Food

These are hard times for working people, with or without families, who want something decent, wholesome, and delicious to eat.

It is not news that our quality of life has been eroded: No one has any time anymore. We race home from work to try and put a meal on the table. Naturally commerce has found a way to help us out of our misery, yet we all know that the food provided us by agribusiness and the food industry is denatured, insufficient, often adulterated, and frequently tasteless. What are we to do?

A person with a job cannot lead the life of a nineteenth-century farm wife who churned her own butter and made her bread from scratch. And what person, with a two-day weekend and possibly a family, wants to spend a Saturday or a Sunday in the kitchen? On the other hand, I do know that the people who are going into the supermarket and buying these things in plastic are not happy. Because when you feed them good food, they all say, "Oh, God, this is *so great*. This is really delicious." And then you say, "This is a cake that took four seconds to make, it was made from scratch by someone who can hardly add two and two. You do not have to go to MIT to make a scratch cake." And they say, "I've never done that. I've just used a mix." And you say, "But if you will just follow these simple directions you will have something excellent, and it will be better than what you have." They've never even thought of it.

It always seems to me that cooking is like love. You don't have to be particularly beautiful or very glamorous, or even very exciting to fall in love. You just have to be interested in it. It's the same thing with food. You do not have to be a genius. You don't have to come from a long culinary tradition. You just have to go to a restaurant and eat a hamburger and say, "This particular hamburger tastes swell." And then you have to say, "Could you please tell me what you did?" And the guy says, "You know, I stuck an ice cube in the meat"—this is an old trick I learned from a cook—"And the bun we got, we got at that bakery on the corner." So you say to yourself, "That tasted wonderful. I will now try to do this in my own kitchen."

You just have to figure out what it is you like: Some people really don't like anchovies, and some people really do. I myself am not particularly interested in restaurant cooking. I don't really want to learn how to make a napoleon. I'd much rather learn how make a very good lemon cake, which you can make in your own home. I like plain, old-fashioned home food. I do not want a three-page recipe. I know a lot of people who started out cooking knowing nothing who instantly went to the most complicated book they could find and did fruit soufflés, with tremendous, disastrous results, when they could easily have done something simple and had a nice time. I think you just have to not get your knickers in a twist.

I did a column for *Gourmet* that featured something called the cooking of the refined slob (see page 70), which is sort of what

I am. It has misty, nostalgic parts about how in the old days I used to make all these butters and put them under the chicken skin and stuff like that. And then I stopped doing all that. And you know what? It did not make one particle of difference. I got a letter from an eighty-five-year-old disabled German lady who still cooked for herself. She said that she cooked exactly as her mother and grandmother had told her, but that she had read my article and had found it very liberating.

So what I say to you is: Never truss a chicken again. That's my hint. I went out and I bought this expensive linen chicken string, and I said to my daughter, "This string was really expensive, okay. We got it in that fancy cooking shop in Litchfield. Don't you dare touch this string, okay? This is for chicken trussing." Well, she made spiderwebs all over the house with that string, and I said to myself, *Who cares? Do I have to do this? I don't have to do this. You don't have to tie up a chicken. Why am I doing this?* And I stopped. Then I stopped doing a lot of other things. You know, the first sentence of Dr. Spock's immortal classic, *Baby and Child Care,* is "Trust yourself." You just have to relax. I assure you that if you keep it simple, everything will turn out just fine.

Adapted from a talk given to the Radcliffe Culinary Friends,
May 17, 1992.

INDEX

Page numbers in *italics* refer to recipes.

ESCAPE WITH **LAURIE COLWIN**

"I've read and reread every book by Laurie Colwin. Acutely observed, beautifully written, witty, and profound—each one is a delight."

—GRETCHEN RUBIN,
author of *Happier at Home* and *The Happiness Project*